10 Steps for Acing the Digital SAT and ACT

The Ultimate Guide for Students and Parents

"One of the things you have to do in life is live up to your damn subtitle."

— Christopher Hitchens

10 Steps for Acing the Digital SAT and ACT

The Ultimate Guide for Students and Parents

Daniel Fischer

Copyright © 2023

www.fasttracktutoringllc.com

All rights reserved. No part of this book may be used or reproduced by any means, graphic, electronic, or mechanical, including photocopying, recording, taping or by any information storage retrieval system without the written permission of the publisher except in the case of brief quotations embodied in critical articles and reviews.

This book is informational and does not guarantee results. The author makes no representations or promises pertaining to a student's score increases. The content and strategies contained herein may not be suitable for your situation.

Client testimonials are used with permission.

Cover Image © DepositPhotos.com

People depicted in stock imagery provided by Deposit Photos are models, and are only used for illustrative purposes.

Author photo by Jess Osber Photography

Prepared for publication by KrystineKercher.com

Cover design by Krystine Kercher

Printed in the United States of America

Dedication

For my father, who gave me my sense of direction. In every sense of the word.

And for my mother, who always reminded me that if I ever won a Tony Award, I would have to thank her in my acceptance speech. Until they create a category for Best Tutor, I hope this dedication will suffice.

"To me, teaching is a sacred profession."

— Stephen Sondheim

Table of Contents

Introduction: The Truth About the SAT and ACT..i

Part I: The Evolving Landscape of Digital Testing

Chapter 1: Why Is Your Test Score So Low – And What You Can Do About It!....................3

Chapter 2: Digital SAT and ACT Overview..13

Chapter 3: How the Digital SAT Sections and Modules Work..................................19

Chapter 4: Why is College Board Doing This?..29

Part II: Creating Your Customized Ten-Step Plan

Chapter 5: To SAT, or to ACT, That is the Question..41

Chapter 6: Wait a Second – Aren't Schools Going Test Optional Now?..54

Chapter 7: Getting to Work – The Months Leading into the Test..59

Chapter 8: The Week Leading into the Test..73

Chapter 9: Knowing When to Retire..79

Chapter 10: Submitting Your Scores..93

Part III: Essential Strategies

Chapter 11: Rapid-Fire Hints..101

Chapter 12: Your Verbal Section Toolbox..106

Chapter 13: Your Math Section Toolbox..126

Part IV: Other Things to Consider

Chapter 14: Ten Myths About the SAT and ACT..139

Chapter 15: Testing with Accommodations..145

Chapter 16: Things We Still Don't Know (For Now)..150

Chapter 17: Maintaining Perspective..153

Acknowledgements..158

Client Testimonials..160

About the Author..163

Introduction: The Truth About the SAT and ACT

"...yeah, we definitely don't see this stuff in school."

– Emily K. (my student during our grammar lesson last week)

The SAT and ACT Do Not Reflect What You're Learning in School

College Board is not telling you the whole truth about the SAT. Here's the truth: what you're learning in high school has very little to do with what you'll see on the SAT.

In their literature, College Board claims that the questions on the SAT reflect the same topics that students see in their high school classes.

This is simply not true.

The ACT is guilty of this as well. In their literature, the ACT folks say that their test measures what you "should have learned by the time you've completed high school".

"Should have" is an interesting choice of words.

Alas, there is no perfect marriage between what students learn in high school and what is considered fair game on the SAT and the ACT.

Just to illustrate with a grammar example, both exams include questions on misplaced modifiers. That's all well and good, but my students from High School A have never seen that topic before. On the math end, both tests include questions on the exponential growth formula. Again, that's fine, but my students from High School B have never learned that formula. (Don't worry, we'll be hitting both of those topics in later chapters!)

I'm going to say it again.

There is no perfect marriage between what students learn in high school and what is considered fair game on the SAT and the ACT.

I don't mean that these exams expect students to know things they have once learned and have since forgotten. *I mean that these exams expect students to know things they have never learned in the first place.*

My students' parents are often incredulous when I tell them this, but it's true.

High School Alone Will Not Prepare Students for the SAT or ACT.

Here is a text I got from a student when she was accepted to college. This was in 2015, when the SAT was about to change from the 2400-scale to the 1600-scale. During that transition, College Board was touting how the material on the updated test would be more aligned with what students saw in their classwork.

She texted me the following:

> "Thank you so much for all you have done for me. I truly hope that the upcoming format changes will be better for the next generation… or that they will at least reflect what we actually learn in high school."

Sadly, that did not happen. Here is a message I got from another student several years later, regarding that updated version of the test:

> "I don't know how anyone knows this material without a tutor!"

And then there's the quote I used at the top of this introduction. In the middle of a recent grammar lesson, a student of mine remarked:

> "…yeah, we definitely don't see this stuff in school."

My students echo these sorts of sentiments every day. Their high school classes have not prepared them for what we see during our SAT and ACT prep.

Now just to be fair, I don't think that College Board or the ACT companies are evil. In this book, I'll give them credit when it's due. And yes, these exams do include *some* topics that my students have seen before.

But when the test makers say that these exams are aligned with what students learn in school, it is simply not true.

Plus, the SAT is about to change from a paper test format to a digital test format.

Are you confused? Nervous? Downright scared?

Then this book is for you! I'm going to give you an exact step-by-step plan for how to prepare for the digital SAT, along with some great strategies for the ACT.

Bridging the Gap

Hello! My name is Daniel, and I have been a professional SAT and ACT tutor for over 20 years. Throughout this book, you'll find testimonials from many of my previous students and their parents. When you're feeling overwhelmed by your test prep, jump around to read some of these success stories. They'll help to keep you motivated.

I'll just include one of these stories here.

Back in 2019, I worked with a student… let's call her Jackie. At first, Jackie was struggling with our lessons. Not academically, but emotionally. More specifically, she was embarrassed to admit when she needed help.

At one of our early lessons, she was stumped on a math question. I asked her, "So what do we do next?" But she was embarrassed to say she didn't know. So we sat in silence for about 25 seconds.

Which was a very long time.

It was like an academic game of chicken. But neither of us budged. Her face got red. I saw tears forming in her eyes. She looked away so she could wipe them.

I put my pencil down and took a deep breath. I told her, "Jackie, it's ok that you don't know what to do. Truly. *But telling me that is one of the best things you can say during our lessons*. It's not just that it will save us time. It will help me understand which step you're confused about. That way, I can help you!" She dried her tears and agreed.

At subsequent lessons, she started to embrace the power of saying, "I don't know." This was a quantum leap forward! And much better than sitting in silence.

All told, her score improved from the 1000's up to 1210, and then up to 1320! When her scores came out, she texted me the following:

> *"Thanks for everything over the past year. I think you're an amazing teacher. Definitely the best I ever had."*

(I'm not crying, you're crying!)

The reason I tell this story – many of my students are hesitant to ask for help. Don't be embarrassed! Admitting that you need help is a crucial first step.

And that's where this book comes in. It is designed to help you bridge the gap between what is not taught in school and what is fair game on these tests.

What You Will Find in This Book

- A complete step-by-step guide for how to prepare for the digital SAT...
- ...along with steps for the ACT!
- Guidance on how to decide which test to focus on.
- A full overview of what you can expect to see on the digital SAT.
- A full analysis of every type of question you'll see on the digital SAT...
- ...along with some killer strategies for each!
- The best test-taking "tricks", tips, and strategies on how to navigate the ACT.

What You Won't Find in This Book

- A coddling approach. I err on the side of tough love. I promise, everything I say stems from a genuine desire to help you achieve your best score. That said, some of what I say might surprise you. (See the next chapter for my speech that shocks all of my students' parents.)
- A false promise of what you can expect for your score increases. See Chapter 9 for a deep dive into what you can expect in terms of reasonable score increases.
- Complicated language or jargon. Yes, the SAT and ACT contain some advanced topics. Still, this book is very user-friendly! Even when addressing some of the most difficult topics, I'll be sure to use clear language that is easy to follow.
- A magical "do-nothing" plan to help your scores go up. Test prep is about more than simple "tricks". There is work involved! Or as a tutoring colleague of mine likes to say:

> "It's a number 2 pencil, not a magic wand."

(That joke is a tad dated now that you don't need a pencil for the digital test. But you get my point.)

My most successful students are those who take ownership over their testing journey. To quote another recent client:

> "Daniel was a great tutor for my daughter. We achieved great results with his help. You get what you put in, and his book will get you started in the right direction!"

I agree! **You get what you put in.** I'll give you great strategies, a detailed road map, and specific step-by-step instructions. But I can't do the work for you. Your success is up to you.

Why Listen to Me?

Just a bit of background:

- For many years, I worked for Kaplan as an SAT and ACT teacher and tutor.
- After a few years, I started training their tutors.
- I then wrote curriculum for the Kaplan product development team.
- I was the writer and host of the cable program *Mastering the SAT*.
- I created the YouTube test prep channel *Plan Your Work – Work Your Plan*. (More on that in a bit.)

But what I'm most proud of is my tutoring company that I've been running for more than a decade. During that time, I've worked with over 1,000 students, helping them achieve their best scores on the SAT and the ACT exams.

And now I'm going to share that secret sauce with you! This book includes the same strategies that I teach my students, along with the same step-by-step plan that I have them follow.

So all of this to say, you're in good hands. Strap in, pour a cup of coffee (is that bad advice for a teenager?), and let's get to work.

"The SAT exam can cause temporary insanity for parents. 'I will find the best prep course for my child.' Thankfully, we found Daniel! Over the course of several years and several children, it seemed like Daniel was our weekly Sunday morning guest. Which timed out well, as I'd often send him home with meatballs and chicken parm.

Kidding. Sort of. But seriously....

Having Daniel was a game changer for my boys. Daniel is a dedicated and outstanding educator. He possesses an innate ability to communicate challenging concepts in a manner children can digest and remember.

But more so, having him in our home was a pleasure as well. On a personal level, he was always kind, honest, reliable, and courteous.

Follow his guidance! Your children's scores will be better for it.

(And send him meatballs. He likes that.)"

— M. P. (Mother of Students from the Classes of 2013 and 2016)

Part I: The Evolving Landscape of Digital Testing

"I scored 1030 on the December 2017 SAT. Daniel helped me improve my score to 1300 on the May 2018 SAT! Follow his advice. His guidance was an essential part of my test day success."

— Jessica H. (Class of 2019)

"Daniel showed me how to break down every type of question on the SAT. His methods helped me go from 1210 on my first SAT to a superscore of 1460! Now that he's sharing these same strategies in his book, take advantage of it."

— Jack E. (Class of 2022)

"Working with Daniel, I was able to improve both my SAT score from 1260 to 1450 and my ACT reading score from 25 to 35!"

— Jack D. (Class of 2022)

In Part I of this book, we'll talk about what you can expect to see on the digital SAT, along with the ACT. Once you're more familiar with the format of each test, we'll move on to action steps in Part II.

But first, let's talk about why you might be surprised by your initial scores.

(And yes, I had both a Jack E. and a Jack D. in the Class of 2022. And just for laughs, they both had sisters named Kate. Really.)

Chapter 1: Why Is Your Test Score So Low – And What You Can Do About It!

"The dream begins with a teacher who believes in you, who tugs and pushes, and leads you on to the next plateau, sometimes poking you with a sharp stick called truth."

— Dan Rather

Let me know if this sounds familiar.

- You just got your PSAT score back... and you can't believe how low it is.
- You just took your first practice ACT... and you're shocked by the low numbers.
- You've been taking a test prep class... but your scores have hit a plateau.

Your immediate reaction is some variation of:

"But my average in school is (insert number here)!"

"But I'm in the A.P. math class!"

"But I take I.B. English!"

My students are often surprised when their SAT and ACT scores don't reflect their grades from high school.

Brace yourself. This might hurt a bit. Your GPA is irrelevant when it comes to the SAT and the ACT.

I'm going to say that again. **Your GPA is irrelevant when it comes to the SAT and the ACT.**

Now, I promise that this book is not all doom and gloom. Rather, my goal is to address the problem so we can find the solution! There is a light at the end of this tunnel.

Let's start by identifying the seven reasons for the discrepancy between your high school grades and your scores on standardized tests.

Reason 1:   Material You've Never Learned Before
Reason 2:   Material You've Learned... But Forgot
Reason 3:   Reading Comprehension Struggles
Reason 4:   Grade Inflation
Reason 5:   Not Thinking Like a Test Taker
Reason 6:   Test-Taking Muscle
Reason 7:   Equity and Access

Let's take a closer look at each.

Reason 1: Material You've Never Learned Before

To reiterate what I said in the Introduction: *there is no perfect marriage between what you see in high school and what is fair game on the SAT and the ACT.*

In the Introduction, I mentioned how many of my students from a certain school have never learned about misplaced modifiers. My students from another high school have never seen the formula for exponential growth. In Chapter 4, I'll make the same point with margin of error. *These are all topics that are fair game on the tests, but many of my students have never seen them before.*

Every state and school district in the country covers different topics of math and English. *No high school class perfectly covers all of the topics you will encounter on the SAT and the ACT.*

This past spring, I was chatting with the mother of one of my sophomore students. She asked me if her daughter should take (fancy name) math class A or (fancy name) math class B in her upcoming junior year. More specifically, she asked me, "Which one would serve her better for the SAT?"

My answer was neither.

Don't pick a math class because you think it will teach you what you need for the SAT! Most of the material from your high school math class will not appear on the SAT. And only a tad more of it will appear on the ACT.

Don't believe me?

Leaf through your junior year math textbook. See how many of those topics overlap with what you'll see on an SAT question.

You'll be hard pressed to find more than a few. Five might be a stretch.

I was recently chatting with one of my students about her upcoming high school math test. I asked her, "Hannah, ballpark, what percent of material from your math class would you say comes up on the SAT?" She said about 15%.

She's not far off.

Now, please don't misinterpret me.

1. I'm not saying that the situation is hopeless! Again, let's diagnose the problem so that we can then move on to the solution.
2. I'm not trying to vilify high schools or teachers. I know many wonderful teachers who are excellent at their job. My mother is one of them. (Hi mom!)

In fact, I don't blame high schools at all. It should not be the responsibility of a high school class to cover the material that is tested on the SAT or the ACT. *It should be the other way! These tests should mirror the material that students see in their everyday classwork.*

But unfortunately, they don't.

Even though both test companies say they do.

For example, this is what the College Board book says when explaining the answer to one of their sample grammar questions. I'm paraphrasing for copyright purposes, but the gist is as follows: "You're probably already familiar with the (such and such) grammar rule."

No, as a matter of fact, many of my students are not familiar with the such and such grammar rule!

A fun anecdote: a student once told me that her English teacher would circle punctuation mistakes in her essays and papers. For example, if she had confused the word *its* and *it's* or *your* and *you're*, the teacher would write things like "This is wrong", or "You need to proofread more". But here's the thing – this student didn't know the difference between those words! So she knew that she had made a mistake, but she didn't know how to correct it. (Shame on that teacher for not explaining those concepts to her, but I digress.)

So when the College Board book says something like, "you probably already understand the concept of subject-verb agreement", the book is wrong! Many of my students have never seen that concept before. And if you're in that same camp of students who have never heard of that topic, that's ok! Keep reading to the end of this chapter.

Let's give the ACT a little love as well. The ACT is notorious for including many math topics that my students have never seen before. For example, the ACT often includes questions on how to multiply two matrices. (Because, you know, that's relevant in life.) However, many of my students have never seen that topic in their math class. Still, the explanation in the ACT book says something like this. Again, I'm paraphrasing for copyright purposes: "...and you might have a math textbook to help explain this example."

Well that's wonderful. But what if you're like my students who have never seen a matrix before? You're screwed. Now what?

Sorry, I'm being flippant. But this sort of language from the test makers infuriates me.

Just to lighten the mood for a moment, you know that scene in the finale of *Breaking Bad...*

> *(What's that? High school students don't watch Breaking Bad? Au contraire! It was actually one of my students who suggested that I should start watching it. And he was right. Good call, Joe! Anyhoo...)*

...where Skylar looks at Walt and says, "If I have to hear you say one more time that you did this for your family!" She's heard him sing that refrain over and over, and she can't bear hearing it one more time.

That's how I feel whenever the SAT and ACT claim that their tests reflect what students see in school. In the words of Dwight Schrute: ***false.***

(Yes, I switched to another TV show reference. Both shows are excellent!
Back to the point...)

Last summer, a student's father came to realize how false these sorts of statements were. After one of our lessons, he commented, "So in this environment of everyone-gets-a-trophy, I guess it's a shock when the kid realizes how much material they don't know."

Bingo!

Now, some of you might now be thinking, "But surely, Daniel, you're not talking about me." Or for the parents reading this, "... that can't be true for my Sally. She attends the such and such high school for gifted children."

Brace yourself. Yes, I'm talking about you.

Or yes, I'm talking about Sally.

Tough love. I know. Stay with me.

Sally – I'm sure that you're a wonderful human being. This doesn't mean that you're not smart. It doesn't mean that you don't have the potential to do well on these tests. This is in no way a personal attack on your character. That said, after 20 years of working with students, I'm confident of this: *your GPA has nothing to do with your SAT and ACT scores. The majority of material that you learn in high school will not appear on either of these tests.*

One more time for the folks in the back: ***there is no perfect marriage between what students learn in high school and what is considered fair game on the SAT and the ACT.***

And that's ok; you're in the right place! This book is designed to help you bridge that gap.

Reason 2: Material You've Learned... But Forgot

To be fair, the SAT and ACT will include *some* material that you've seen before. However, it is usually material that you haven't seen in years.

Often, when my students get stuck on an SAT or ACT math question, it's not because they don't understand the advanced 11th grade math topic that's in play. Rather, it's because they've forgotten a much more fundamental concept. For example, a student recently told me that she knew how to simplify a derivative in her math class, but she still missed a practice SAT question because she'd forgotten how to divide fractions.

I see this sort of thing with my students constantly; they know the schmancy 11th grade topic, but they've forgotten the simpler (9th... 7th... 5th) grade topic that the question is testing.

And these simpler topics are the bread-and-butter of the test!

Reason 3: Reading Comprehension Struggles

About 10 years ago, I worked with a student who struggled mightily on the verbal sections. Still, she had a high GPA. I asked her, "Chloe..." (her name was not Chloe), "Chloe... when you read a book for school, give me a ballpark number... what percentage of it do feel like you understand? 80%? 50%?"

She told me – without sarcasm – that she had never read a book.

Yep. Just another honor roll student.

After my pulse started again, I asked her how she maintained her grades in her English class. She told me that she listened to the classroom discussions, took notes on what the teacher said, and found online summaries for whatever they were reading. That was enough to get by.

And now here she was, being asked to read complex college-level SAT reading passages.

And she didn't understand a word.

Chloe is not an anomaly. Your grades in English class are not a leading indicator of how you might score on your SAT and ACT verbal sections.

How do we combat that? We'll get there in future chapters!

Reason 4: Grade Inflation

Then there is grade inflation. Back in my day (wow, did I just say that??), it was not common for students to hold a GPA above a 90, and even less common for students to hold a GPA above a 95. These days, everyone has a high GPA.

In a recent press release, College Board said the following:

> *"While high school grades are an important reflection of students' work, the share of students graduating from high school with an A average has grown from 39% in 1998 to 55% in 2021."*

They even use this data point to market their test! In October of 2022, I saw a College Board ad pop up on my computer that said this:

> "Most college freshmen were 'A' students in high school. Don't miss the chance to stand out! (And then an advertisement to take the upcoming December SAT.)"

And they're right! They know that the majority of students are applying to colleges with high GPAs. A high GPA does not help you stand out the way it once did.

A student recently told me how her GPA was calculated. Students in the I.B. or A.P. classes have their grades multiplied by a certain factor. So, students scoring in the high 70's have their numbers bumped to the low 90's. Students scoring in the low 80's have their numbers bumped to the high 90's, and so on.

As a result, some of my students, and their parents, have an inaccurate sense of their strengths and weaknesses. Their grades do not indicate how much they might be struggling with a certain topic.

Plus, there's the partial credit factor. If students do just one thing wrong on a math test question in school, their teacher might still give them 9 out of 10 points. Alas, no luck with that on the SAT or the ACT! These tests will either reward you the full point or they won't. There is no partial credit for doing five out of six things correctly within a question.

And one parent even told me how her daughter had her grade bumped a bit for attendance, behavior, and "just being nice". That's all well and good, but no such luck with that on the SAT or the ACT.

A Brief Aside: There is No "Should"

Here's an exchange I once had with a student after her second attempt at the SAT. She had seen some solid math jumps, but her verbal numbers had hit a plateau.

Me – How was the reading section for you?

Her – I feel like I should be scoring higher there.

Me – Good to know. Why do you say that? Do you feel that you understand the passages, and you're then getting tripped up on the questions?

Her – ...no.

Me – Ok. Are you understanding the passages, but then struggling with the timing factor?

Her – ...no.

Me – Ok. So... why do you say that you should be scoring higher there?

Her – ... *I just feel like I should be!*

Says who?

And I promise, I liked this student! I'm lovingly picking on her here. Still, she thought her stellar high school grades meant she "should be" scoring higher on the SAT.

Nope.

Now, I'm not saying a high GPA means you *can't* score well on the SAT or the ACT. After all, that's why we're here! But don't think that having a certain GPA means you *should* have a certain standardized test score.

And the flip side of that is also true! *Just as a high GPA does not mean you should do well on the SAT or the ACT, a low GPA does not mean you shouldn't do well on the SAT or ACT!* There is little correlation between the two.

The strategies and methods outlined in this book can help students from any GPA improve their SAT and ACT scores. As I said in the Introduction, it's all up to you!

But your GPA is not a leading indicator of your potential to do well on these tests, nor is it a leading indicator of your potential to do poorly.

Reason 5: Not Thinking Like a Test Taker

Many of my students are not used to thinking the way that the SAT and ACT want them to think. Here's an example of the type of thinking that stumps many of my students.

Q. The number of bacteria on a lake will double every day. The bacteria will reach their final amount on the 30th day. On what day will the bacteria reach half of that final amount?

Take a minute to think about an answer before you keep reading.

(I'll pause to let you work on it. Writing this chapter is making me hungry. Should I make a panini or an omelet on my lunch break?)

9 out of 10 times, my students will say that the answer is 15. Or more accurately, 5 out of 10 will say 15, and 4 out of 10 will say, "I don't know."

Let's consider 15. That's logical, right? Half the time must mean half the number. So if we're hitting the final number on the 30th day, then the 15th day must be half of that amount. Right? RIGHT?!?

But that's linear thinking. If you're doubling something forever, that's not linear growth; that's exponential growth.

Let's use actual numbers to make this idea more concrete. Let's say that we're starting with 2 bacteria, because why not. (And don't worry, we won't do this 30 times. But let's pretend we're going to.)

On day 1, we have 2 bacteria. Doubling that...

On day 2, we have 4 bacteria. So far so good. Doubling that...

On day 3, we have 8 bacteria. Continuing to double...

Day 4 would be 16...

Day 5 would be 32...

And so on... and so on... and so on...

Notice – every day is *half* of the day that follows it. Day 1 was half of day 2. Day 2 was half of day 3. This will continue forever. Day 11 will be half of day 12... day 23 will be half of day 24... and so on...

...until day 29 is half of day 30. The answer is 29! If the bacteria doubles on day 29, you'll arrive at the final number for day 30. This means that day 29 is half the amount of day 30.

Aha! Now that you got it, let's do it again. Let's say you have the same situation: bacteria are doubling every day. But now, they're going to reach their final number on the 72nd day, because why not. On what day will the number of bacteria reach half of that amount?

(I'll pause to let you think about it... and I think we're going with an omelet.)

Just like before, it's doubling every day. This means that the 71st day will have half of the number of the 72nd day. The answer is 71. (And just like 15 being the trap answer on the first question, 36 would be the trap answer here. Half the time does not mean half the amount!)

Now, some of my students understand that first question instantly. They can immediately tell me that the answer is 29. But other students, most of my students in fact, absolutely need the explanation above.

And if you needed the explanation too, that's ok! But that illustrates the point: *there is a difference between high school-based computation and test-based critical thinking.*

Many of my students are not used to this.

(And now I'm back after eating. It was delicious.)

The Reason You Really Want Me to Include: "Just a Bad Test Taker"

At this point, most of you are (hopefully) with me. For the students, you're thinking, "You're right! They don't ask us questions like this in school." Or for the parents, you're thinking, "We're so glad we found this book for Charlie!" Hi Charlie. Glad to have you here.

But for some of you, I can still hear your gears grinding. You want to say something like, "Daniel, you're still not talking about Sally. She's a good student! *She's just a bad test taker."*

Are there students with genuine learning struggles? Of course. I have had many students with learning disabilities, I.E.P.s and 504 plans. This chapter is not intended to diminish how those struggles can indeed impact a student's test-taking experience. (See Chapter 15 on testing with accommodations.)

Still, all too often, I hear the parents of my students say, "... she's very smart, she's just a bad test taker."

Sometimes. *But sometimes, she just doesn't know the material.*

And it is critical to be able to make that distinction.

Reason 6: Test-Taking Muscle

And there are many other factors in play as well, such as timing struggles (especially on the ACT), energy, stamina, focus, nerves, and test-taking anxiety.

These factors, along with countless others, help to explain why a student with a GPA of (insert high number *x*) might have a standardized test score of (insert low number *y*). It is not the exception to the rule; it happens for many students.

Reason 7: Equity and Access

And finally, there are issues of equity and access. Not every student has the same access to quality education. And certainly, even fewer students have access to elite test prep. Tutors and prep classes can be prohibitively expensive. Not every family can "afford a Daniel".

That's why I created this book! I wanted to remove that barrier. This book covers the same "secret sauce" that I teach my students.

And it's also why I created my YouTube channel, which is completely free and available to everyone!

My channel is called *Plan Your Work – Work Your Plan*. It is an invaluable resource for your test prep! (Side note – invaluable means extremely valuable. My students hate that one.)

The videos on my channel cover the same lessons that I teach my students. Here's how to incorporate those videos with this book.

How to Incorporate My YouTube Channel with this Book

My YouTube channel, and this book, are designed to bridge the gap between what is not taught in school and what these tests want you to know.

Whenever I mention a specific topic, I'll include a link to my YouTube video that covers that lesson. So if I mention a topic that you're not familiar with, go watch that video!

For example, earlier in this chapter, I mentioned subject-verb agreement. If you don't know what that is, check it out here! This video contains my full lesson on that topic.

https://tinyurl.com/DanFisch1

Or for those on the ACT path, I mentioned earlier how the ACT might ask you to multiply two matrices. If you have no idea how to do that, go to this video! I cover that topic in full detail.

https://tinyurl.com/DanFisch2

This book will cover some essential test-taking strategies. From there, I'll cover *some* material. But when needed, I'll include the link to the video that covers that topic in more detail.

My YouTube channel is an outstanding supplement to this book. **More so – it is designed to bridge the gap between what is not taught in high school and what is fair game on the test.**

And that is how to overcome the discrepancy between your GPA and your standardized test scores.

Now, before we get to actual material, let's start with an overview of what you'll see on each test. Once you're more familiar with the format, we can get to a step-by-step plan.

Chapter 2: Digital SAT and ACT Overview

*"If you know the enemy and you know yourself,
you need not fear the result of a hundred battles."*

— Sun Tzu

What Will Be Covered in this Chapter

- So what is the digital SAT?
- How will it differ from its paper test predecessor?
- How will it be the same?
- What can you expect to see on it?
- What is the format of the ACT?
- And what about the ACT going digital?

A Quick Disclaimer

Suffice it to say, this is a fluid situation. College Board is announcing more about the digital SAT every day. All of the information in this book reflects what we know at the time of this publication.

Refer to my website www.fasttracktutoringllc.com for the most recent information regarding any updates to the test season. I'll keep you posted as things evolve.

But as of now, here's what we know. Let's start with the digital SAT. Then we'll talk about the ACT.

What We Know About the Digital SAT

College Board is not simply going to offer the previous paper SAT on a digital platform; the questions on the digital SAT will be wholly different from those that appeared on the paper test.

Students will take the digital SAT on a computer, laptop, or tablet. To address issues of inequity, College Board is ensuring that all students will have the same opportunities to take the test. So if students don't have their own device, College Board will provide one. (Put a point on the board of me giving them credit where they deserve it!)

Students will have to take the test at a school or another testing center. So even though they can take the test on their own device, alas, they can't take the test at home. They'll still need to go to a testing location with a proctor.

Before taking the test, they'll need to download the digital testing application. Once they get to the test center, they'll use that application to access the test. The application is designed to disable other web access to prevent possible cheating. In Chapter 8, I cover the details of what to do to download this application.

Anticipating Technical Glitches

College Board has anticipated the technical glitches that might come up during the test. For example, what happens if the Wi-Fi cuts out? Or what if your computer battery dies in the middle of a section? Don't panic! If something goes wrong, the test will retain all of the work that you've done up to that point. You won't lose any of your answers and you won't lose any time from a section. Once you're able to return to the test, you'll be able to resume where you left off. (Tally another point in the column of me giving College Board credit where it's due!)

Timeline of the Rollout – A Clean Break

- November of 2021: College Board piloted the digital SAT for select students. This was a "trial run", where they offered the digital test to a small number of schools.
- January of 2022: College Board officially announced how the digital test would roll out in different stages.
- March of 2023: the digital test replaced the paper test for international students outside of the U.S.
- October of 2023: the digital PSAT replaced the paper PSAT.
- Spring of 2024: the digital SAT will replace the paper SAT in the U.S.

At that point, College Board will make a clean break to the digital format. Starting in 2024, students in the U.S. will only be able to take the test digitally.

However, some students have testing accommodations that specifically require a paper test. Those students will still be able to take the test on paper. For everyone else, the test will be digital.

What is Changing vs. What is Staying the Same?

The digital SAT is still scored out of 1600 and covers the same content areas as the previous paper test: reading, grammar, and math. However, the digital test doesn't just deliver the paper test format on a digital platform. The format and question types are changing considerably.

- The digital test is shorter. The paper test was a bit over 3 hours (and longer still with the optional essay), while the new test is a bit over 2 hours.
- The reading passages on the digital test are much shorter. On the paper test, the passages were 5 or 6 paragraphs long, with up to 12 questions per passage. On the digital test, the passages are only 1 or 2 paragraphs, with only 1 question per passage.
- Because the passages are shorter, there are more of them. As such, these passages will pull from more varied topics. College Board is trying to use this as a selling point that students will now find the passages more engaging. I'll let you all be the judge of that. (Or put another way, I'll still have students who will hate the reading section, no matter what topics the passages cover.)
- The reading passages may now include poetry excerpts.
- The digital test has several built-in tools: a calculator, a timer (which students can hide), and a reference table for certain math rules.
- Speaking of the calculator, students are allowed to use a calculator on the entire math test. On the paper test, students were only allowed to use a calculator on one of the two math sections. Also, students can use their own calculator if they prefer, or the calculator tool that is embedded in the test.
- Students can "flag" a question as one that they'd like to come back to.
- Students can "strike out" any answer choices that they wish to eliminate.
- Students can use paper for scratch work, but the test also includes an annotation tool.

So those are some of the technical changes coming to the digital test. But the biggest change is that the digital test is going to be computer-adaptive.

What does that mean?

Computer-Adaptive

Computer-adaptive means that the test will "adapt" as students take it. So students won't necessarily see the same questions as others who are taking the same test! Their performance on an earlier section determines what they'll see on a later section.

This is called computer-adaptive. Or more specifically, section-adaptive. Here's how it works.

The verbal and math sections are broken up into two portions called "modules". The first module is called "the routing module" because it "routes them" or decides which path they will see in their second module.

If students do better on the first module, they'll see a harder second module. If they don't do as well on the first module, they'll see an easier second module.

Because of that, students will only see one module at a time. When working on a module, they can answer the questions in any order. However, they'll have to complete their work on the first module before they can move on to the second module. Why? Because their performance on the first module determines what they'll see in the second module. Likewise, once they begin their second module, they cannot return to the first module.

This is very different from the paper SAT, which was a static linear test. On that exam, everyone saw the same questions. (Well, more specifically, everyone saw the same questions, but those questions were shuffled in a different order. So one student's question 12 might have been someone else's question 15. College Board did this to prevent cheating. Still, by the end of a section, everyone saw the same questions.)

But this will not be the case on the digital SAT; the questions can vary from student to student. This is especially true on the second module, where one student might be routed to the easier module, and another might be routed to the harder module.

So don't cheat! On the ethics side, because that would be wrong. On the practical side, because it won't help. The student next to you won't necessarily see the same questions that you see. So keep your eyes on your own screen.

This section-adaptive format might sound stressful, but it offers two very nice benefits:

1. It enables College Board to pinpoint your scores more quickly. This is why the new test is shorter than its paper predecessor.
2. It also lets College Board release your scores more quickly.

Faster Scores

Students who took the paper SAT would typically see their scores 13 days after they took the exam. This was not a guarantee, but usually, the scores would be posted two Fridays after the exam.

College Board says that the digital test will shorten that timeline to "a matter of days".

That would be great!

That said, I had students outside of the United States take the digital SAT in the spring, summer, and fall of 2023. Those scores still took 13 days to appear online.

Granted, these were the very first digital tests to be given. So it's certainly possible College Board will improve its systems and shorten this timeline moving forward. We shall see!

SAT Scoring

The digital test will still be scored on the same scale as the paper test. The verbal and math scores will still range from 200 – 800, with a final score ranging from 400 – 1600. However, each "path" caps you at a certain number.

Students on the harder path can earn up to the full 800 per section. Students on the lower path will be capped at a lower number. And what are those numbers? At the time of this writing, we don't know.

See Chapter 10 for some guidelines on how to submit your scores to colleges, including details on superscoring, Score Choice, etc. See Chapter 16 for my thoughts on superscoring between the paper test and the digital test.

SAT Timing and Availability

For the paper exam, schools were limited as to when they could offer the test. However, the digital test will be offered on dates that are convenient for the school. This should offer more testing flexibility.

ACT Format and Scoring

Some students are very good candidates for the SAT, while others are better candidates for the ACT. But how do you know which test to pursue? Check out Chapter 5! I do a deep dive into how to decide which test is the better fit for you. There are pros and cons for each.

But just a quick overview: the ACT also includes questions on reading, grammar, and math. However, that test is still given as a paper and pencil exam. Plus, the ACT has that weird science section. (Spoiler alert – it's not testing science! See my video here for some great tips on how to move through the ACT science section.)

https://tinyurl.com/DanFisch3

The sections on the ACT appear as follows:

English – 45 minutes

Math – 60 minutes

Reading – 35 minutes

Science – 35 minutes

Each section is graded on a scale of 1 to 36. The final score is taken from the average of your scores on each section, and then rounds to the nearest whole number.

Again, check out Chapter 5, where I talk about how to decide which test is the right fit for you. Also check out Chapter 10, where I talk about how the superscoring option works for the ACT.

Is a Digital ACT on the Way?

At the time of this publication, there are no plans for the ACT to go digital.

Well, slight clarification there: the ACT *does* offer a digital version of their exam. However, *the digital ACT test is identical to the current paper ACT test; it's just offered on a digital platform.* In other words, it's the same test. You'll just take it on a computer instead of in a test booklet.

These digital ACTs are only offered to a small handful of schools. When signing up for the ACT, my students have recently seen a message about an online ACT being available in certain areas.

At the time of this writing, there are no plans for the ACT to completely overhaul its format. We will see how they react to the new digital SAT! Check out my website at www.fasttracktutoringllc.com, and I'll keep you posted if the ACT announces anything on this front.

So that's the big picture of the format for each test. Now let's get to the nitty gritty of how the modules work within the computer-adaptive test.

Chapter 3: How the Digital SAT Sections and Modules Work

"Daniel helped me 'de-code' each question, which helped me know exactly what to expect on the test. With his help, I was able to improve from 1220 on the March 2018 SAT to 1370 on the November 2018 SAT. These scores helped me earn a Presidential Scholarship of $22,000 a year at Loyola. Follow his guidance! It's like going to the 'gym' for your SAT score."

— Kevin M. (Class of 2019)

Let's start with the basic structure of the sections on the **digital SAT**. Then we'll zoom in to see how the modules work within those sections.

Basic Structure of Each Section

The digital SAT is split into 2 sections: verbal and math. **Each of those sections is split into 2 modules.**

Don't memorize any of this, but purely by the numbers....

Each verbal module contains 27 questions, so the **full verbal section is made up of 54 total verbal questions. Each module lasts 32 minutes, combining to 64 minutes for the full verbal section.**

Each math module contains 22 questions, so the **full math section is made up of 44 total math questions. Each module lasts 35 minutes, combining to 70 minutes for the full math section.**

Again, the first module is called the "routing" module; your performance on your first verbal and math modules will determine what you'll see in your second verbal and math modules. More on that in a bit.

Within each section, College Board categorizes their questions into what they call "domains". Here's an overview of what you'll see in each.

Question Domains

The verbal questions are split into 4 different domains.

Domain 1: Craft and Structure
Domain 2: Information and Ideas
Domain 3: Standard English Conventions
Domain 4: Expression of Ideas

The first two domains make up your reading score. The second two domains make up your writing score. In Chapter 12, we'll do a deep dive into all of the verbal questions that you'll see!

The math questions are split into 4 domains as well.

Domain 1: Algebra
Domain 2: Advanced Math
Domain 3: Geometry and Trigonometry
Domain 4: Problem Solving and Analysis

In Chapter 13, we'll talk about some killer math strategies!

Now let's talk about how the questions are arranged within the modules.

"Daniel possesses a great deal of knowledge about these tests, but in his personalized approach, he was always able to explain the concepts in a way that made sense to our daughter. She would often tell us how Dan's approach was far different from that of other tutors. As such, there was always a sense of trust in the process. He really took the time to get to know our daughter, and us! We couldn't be happier about her incredible score jumps. And we couldn't be happier about finding Daniel! Follow his guidance."

— Emily's Parents (Class of 2024)

Order of the Questions

Format of the Verbal Modules

Reading

| 1 | 2 | 3 | 4 | 5 | 6 | 7 | 8 | 9 | 10 | 11 | 12 | 13 | 14 |

☐ Easy
■ Medium
■ Hard
☐ Unscored

Craft and Structure
- Words in Context
- Text Structure and Purpose
- Cross-Text Connections

Info and Ideas
- Central Ideas and Details
- Command of Evidence
- Inferences

Writing

| 15 | 16 | 17 | 18 | 19 | 20 | 21 | 22 | 23 | 24 | 25 | 26 | 27 | 28 |

Standard English Conventions
- Boundaries
- Form, Structure, and Sense

Expression of Ideas
- Transitions
- Rhetorical Synthesis

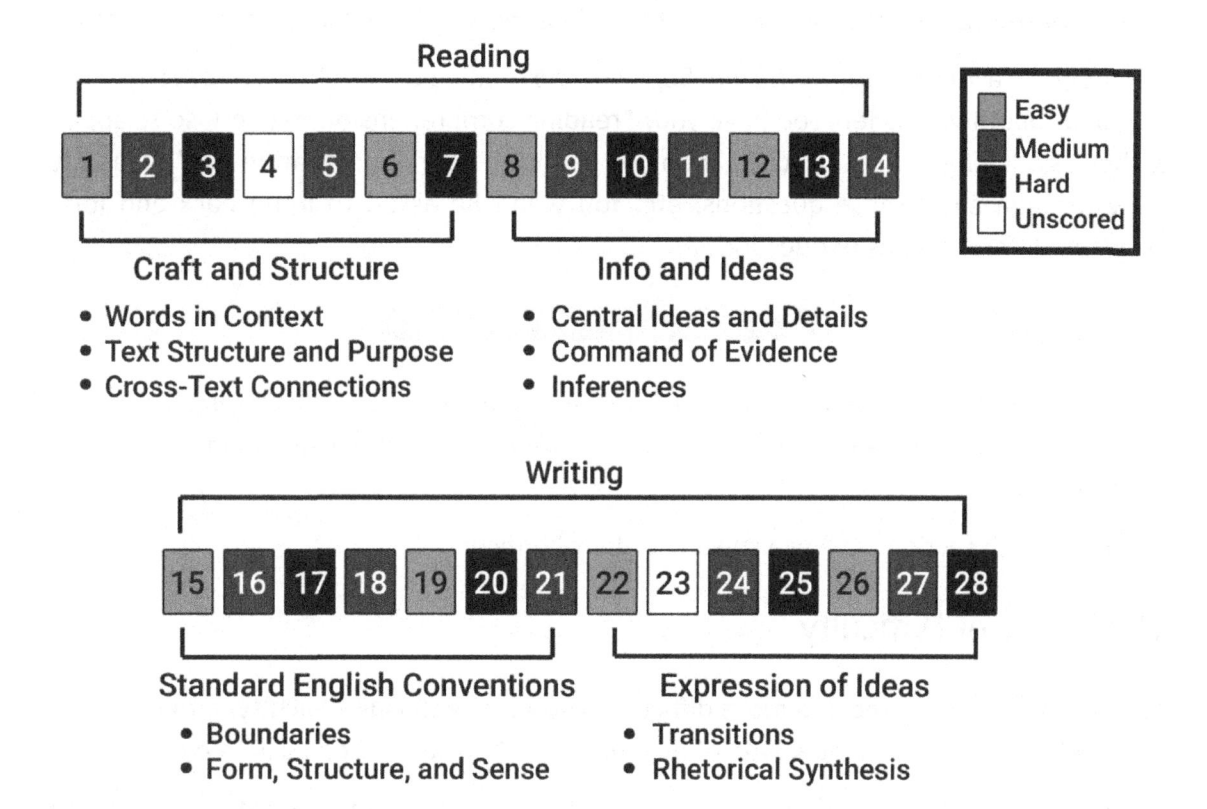

Figure 1

Let's start with the verbal modules.

The first half of each verbal module covers the two domains that will make up your reading score: Craft and Structure, and Info and Ideas. In Figure 1, the question types are listed under each domain (Words in Context, Text Structure and Purpose, etc.). Again, we'll cover all of these questions in Chapter 12!

The second half of each verbal module covers the two domains that will make up your writing score: Standard English Conventions, and Expression of Ideas. And likewise, in Chapter 12, we'll dig into those questions (Boundaries, Transitions, etc.).

Now here's an interesting feature about the digital test: the verbal question types will appear in "clumps". For example, at the beginning of any module, all of the Words in Context questions will appear together.

And this is the case with all of the verbal questions. All of the Transition questions will appear together, just as all of the Rhetorical Synthesis questions will appear together, etc.

This is very different from the paper SAT and the current ACT. On those tests, the verbal questions were (and are) shuffled. In other words, on the ACT grammar section, you might see a "quick fix" punctuation question, followed by a longer organization question, followed by a transition question, followed by another "quick fix" punctuation question.

This is not the case on the digital test, where all of the similar questions appear together.

This helps to avoid *context switching*. So, all of the reading comprehension questions are grouped together. This lets you have your "reading comprehension hat" on, so to speak, without switching to another task. Then you can have your "punctuation hat" on as you plow through all of those questions, etc. You won't be asked to jump back and forth between different types of questions.

In the math module, the questions are not grouped together by category. So in that section, you might see an algebra question, followed by a geometry question, followed by another algebra question, etc.

However, both sections follow a specific order of difficulty.

The Order of Difficulty

The verbal questions become more difficult as you move through each type of question. Then, when you start the new type of question, they'll reset and go back to easy.

In Figure 1, this is indicated by the darker shading. Notice how the questions get darker within each question type, and then they go back to lighter.

This is called a "sawtooth" pattern of difficulty. Each type of verbal question ramps up in difficulty, and then resets back to easy when the new type of question starts.

Format of the Math Modules

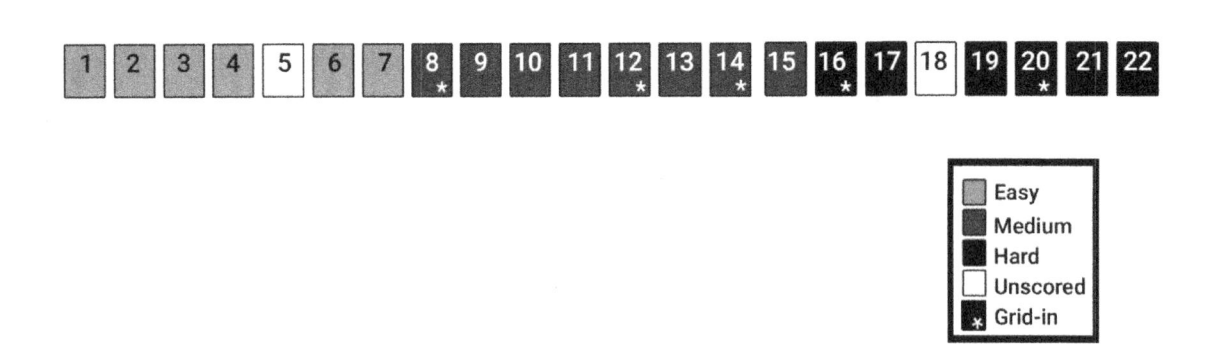

Figure 2

The math questions also appear in order of difficulty. However, they don't follow the same "sawtooth" pattern as the verbal questions. Rather, the math questions escalate in difficulty from the start of the module through the end of the module. In Figure 2, notice how the shading gets darker from the beginning of the section to the end of the section.

Now, you might be asking, what's the deal with those unshaded boxes that are labeled "unscored"? Good eye!

Unscored Questions

In both Figure 1 and Figure 2, notice that several boxes don't have any shading. These questions are unscored. Somewhere in your verbal module will be two questions that do not count towards your score. Likewise with two questions within each math module.

College Board is testing these questions for the future. They use the language "pretesting" for the questions that don't count, and "operational" for the questions that do count. However, you'll have no way of knowing which are which during your exam. So, just treat every question like it counts, even though two of them won't.

Why do they do this? To make sure that you actually try on these questions. This helps them collect more accurate data.

Just to go back in time for a moment: back on the 2400-scale SAT that was retired in 2016, there was actually a *full experimental section!* This was a full 25-minute section where the questions did not count. However, students had no way of knowing which section that was, so they had to try their best on every section. 25 minutes of their life wasted.

On the paper test that was just retired, section 5 was the experimental section. This essentially told students that they didn't have to take section 5 seriously. This made it very difficult for College Board to collect reliable data on these questions.

So the digital test is taking a different approach: it sprinkles in two "pretest" questions within each module. But students have no way of knowing which questions they are. This ensures that students will give all questions their full effort, which helps College Board collect more accurate data.

Long story short – you won't know which questions are the pretest questions, so just treat every question like it counts.

But if there's a killer question that you really hate, cross your fingers; it might not count towards your score!

Grid-In Questions

Also, look back at Figure 2 for a moment. Notice that certain boxes have stars in the bottom right corner. These represent the student-produced response questions, or the "grid-in" questions.

There are two types of SAT math questions: multiple choice and grid-ins. Multiple choice questions will list four possible answers after each question, labeled A through D. The grid-in questions will not list answer choices; instead, these questions will ask you to bubble in your own number. So if the answer is 137, you would actually bubble in the digits 1, 3, and 7.

In Chapter 11, I'll cover the specific instructions for the grid-in questions.

Discrete Questions

Unlike the paper SAT, the digital test uses *discrete questions* on both the verbal and math sections.

(Let's just sort out the words discrete vs. discreet for a moment. Because vocab, why not?)

Discrete means separate or distinct. Discreet means subtle or sneaky.

So when we talk about the test using *discrete* questions, we're talking about the questions being separate from each other. We're not talking about questions being sneaky or inconspicuous.

You good? We good. Back to the point.

On the paper SAT, students would have seen a much longer reading passage. Each passage was followed by 10 to 12 questions. This is not the case on the digital SAT. The reading passages on the digital SAT are only a paragraph (or two paragraphs for the Cross-Text Connections). Each passage is then followed by only one question. This is what they mean by discrete questions; each passage will only contain one question. Other literature refers to them as "stand alone questions".

Likewise for the math. On the paper SAT, some of the math questions used to come in "sets". A word problem could have been followed by two or three related questions. The digital test is doing away with this. There will be only one question per prompt.

This offers several benefits.

First, it's nice for the attention span factor! Students can "get in and get out", without getting bored by an impossibly long passage. (The passages are not necessarily easier, mind you. Just shorter.)

This also helps College Board to prevent cheating, since you won't stay on the same screen for too long.

Another nice perk of this format is that a super-tough reading passage can't tank your score! So if there's a passage you absolutely hate, no big deal. It will only be followed by one question. It's not like the old test, where a killer passage might have brought 12 questions down with the ship.

Also, the math questions are more streamlined to remove the "fluff" from the wording. Again, this doesn't mean that these shorter math questions are easier. They just won't ask you to sift through chunks of extraneous information.

Now let's get to the fun part: what happens when you move from one module to the next.

Moving to the Second Modules

As we said, your performance on your first module will determine what you'll see on your second module.

This is true for both the verbal and the math, but let's use a math module to illustrate.

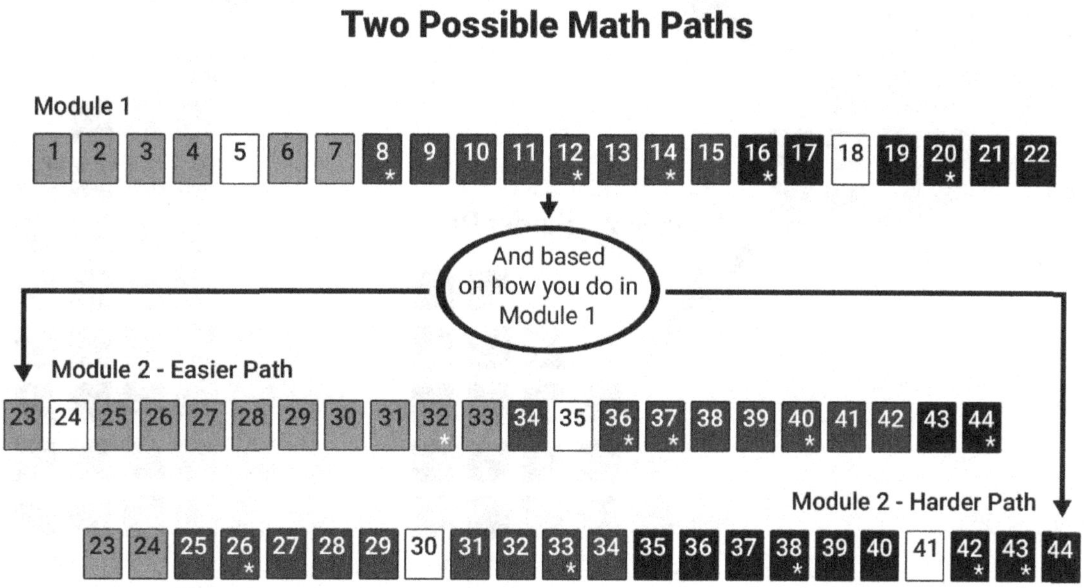

Two Possible Math Paths

Figure 3

After students take the first math module, the test will "route them" to the easier or the harder second math module. In Figure 3, notice that the easier path has more lightly shaded questions, while the harder path has more darkly shaded questions. However, both the easy path and the harder path contain a mix of easy, medium, and hard questions.

So let's look at the totals for each path.

Module 1
5 10 5

Module 2 - Easier Path
10 7 3

Module 2 - Harder Path
3 7 10

Easier Path Totals
15 17 8

Harder Path Totals
8 17 15

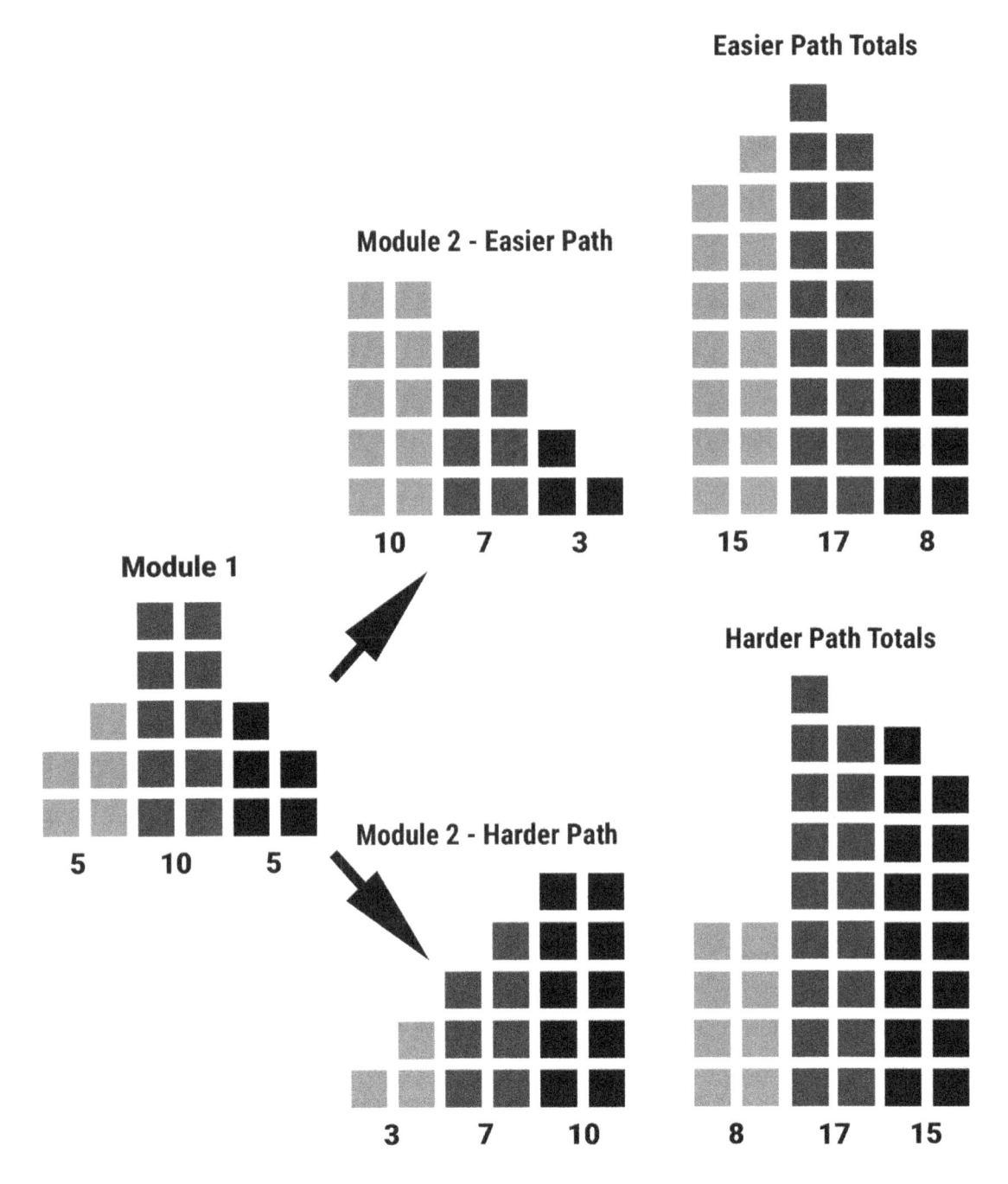

Figure 4

Both paths contain the same number of medium-level questions. It's the number of easies and hards that vary between them.

(And my computer doesn't like that I'm making those words into plural nouns. Meh, I'm going with it.)

What Does This Mean for the Scoring?

I'll cut to the chase – don't worry about it.

Really.

Don't worry about it.

But if you insist...

Yes, it's true that to earn the highest scores, you would need to be on the harder module path. So doesn't it matter?

Not necessarily. You can still achieve the majority of scores on either path.

Don't go into it with a mindset that you *must* make the cutoff for the harder path. Do as well as you can on whatever module you see. And if you see easier questions, good! Rack up on them. Or to use a basketball analogy, rack up on the lay-ups and don't worry about sinking all of the 3-pointers.

Also (more tough love coming), *if you should not be in the harder second module, you would not want to be. Your potential for a higher score could actually come from the easier module.* Or put more bluntly, *you might get your ass kicked in the harder module.* It is extremely unlikely that someone who shouldn't be in the harder second module would then "run the table" on that set of harder questions. So it could actually be a blessing not to wind up in the harder module!

Or back to the basketball analogy: instead of missing the 3-pointers, clean up on the lay-ups. (And for those who don't follow the sports ball, instead of missing all of the hardest questions, clean up on the low-hanging fruit.)

This can also carry a psychological advantage. On the paper test, some students might have felt out of their depth throughout an entire section. By the time they were halfway in, they might have just sighed, thrown their hands up in defeat, and then spent the rest of the section having a pity party.

On the easier module path, they won't be discouraged so easily! Instead, they're now likely to see many more questions that are in their wheelhouse. This will hopefully help to keep them engaged throughout the full module.

On the flip side, if you should be in the harder second module, you'll likely get there with any sort of effort. Just as it is very unlikely that a student in the lower percentile would be routed to the harder path, it is equally unlikely that a student in the top percentile would be routed to the easier path.

So what exactly is the cutoff? The exact details are unclear. It appears that you would need to get a bit more than two-thirds of the questions right from the first module to move on to the harder second module. But this varies from test to test.

And where does the easier module cap your score? Again, as of this writing, we don't know.

Item Response Theory (I.R.T.)

How does College Board calculate this? The new test uses something called *Item Response Theory*, or I.R.T.

College Board has not been entirely clear on how this is going to work. But the basic idea is this: on the paper SAT, as well as the current ACT, questions were (and are) weighted equally. Your final score was calculated by simply tallying how many right and wrong answers you had. The easier questions were worth just as much as the harder ones.

So let's make up an extreme example with the current ACT. The ACT math section has 60 math questions, which get harder as they go. Let's pretend that you answer questions 1 – 30 correctly and questions 31 – 60 incorrectly. You would get the same exact score as someone who hypothetically answered questions 1-30 incorrectly and questions 31 – 60 correctly. (Improbable as that is, given that those later questions are harder, but you get my point. The harder questions are not weighted more than the easier questions.)

This is not necessarily the case with I.R.T. Different questions could be weighted differently. So students with an identical tally of right and wrong answers might not earn the same final score.

All of that said, **do not let this change your testing behavior.**

And don't engage in any sort of gamesmanship to "slow-play" the first section (we've moved from basketball analogies to poker analogies) to then be routed to the easier second module. You're playing with fire! Do as well as you can with whatever questions you see.

Plus, **you won't know which module path you're in during your test!** Don't let thoughts creep in like, "These questions seem far too easy… I guess I didn't make the cutoff for the harder path… I must be on the easier path… damn… I'm screwed."

Put all of the above out of your mind and do your best on whatever questions you see. Easier said than done, of course. **But truly, worrying about which path you're on will only distract you. Just do the best you can on whatever questions you see. The impact of I.R.T. is not as consequential as you think.**

So, you can see how different the digital test is from its paper test predecessor. Why is College Board even doing this in the first place? Read on! Then we'll get to a specific step-by-step plan.

Chapter 4: Why is College Board Doing This?

"It's a bit of a nothing burger."

— The best line I've heard about the digital test.

Now that you're more familiar with the format of the digital SAT, you might be asking yourself, "Why is College Board making this change? What's the point?"

(Granted, you might have been asking yourself before we even started.)

But seriously, why would College Board go through such a major overhaul of the SAT?

There are four main reasons for this. I agree with... two and a half of them. But according to College Board, they are transitioning to the digital test because it is:

1 — Easier to take
2 — Easier to give
3 — More secure
4 — More relevant

For those who paid attention to the first few chapters, you'll know that I think that point number 4 is utter nonsense. But points 1, 2, and 3 are valid. Let's take a look at each.

1 – Easier to Take

This is the point I'll "half-agree" with. As we mentioned earlier, the digital test will be about an hour shorter than the paper test. College Board is touting this as a selling point for students. So yes, the digital test is less of a mental marathon.

Also, I mentioned how College Board removed a lot of the "fluff" from the math questions. The wording of these questions will now be more streamlined. However, that doesn't mean that the math questions will be easier; they will just contain less extraneous information.

Reading passages will be streamlined as well. They will be one paragraph, instead of six or seven. So, that's good for shorter attention spans. College Board also claims that because the passages will pull from more varied topics, students will find them "more interesting". As I said in a previous chapter, I'll let you all be the judge of that. (More to the point, there will still be students who will hate the reading passages with every fiber of their being.)

And of course, some students might prefer taking the test digitally instead of on paper. We all live our lives digitally, from the way we consume entertainment to the way we interact with friends and family. To that point, students might enjoy the "choreography" of the digital test over that of the paper test. We shall see!

2 – Easier to Give

For this point, I'll fully agree! The digital platform makes it much easier for College Board to deliver the test.

The paper test opened the door to many potential security risks:

- Delivering the test to the school.
- Storing and handling the test.
- Proctoring the test correctly.
- Collecting the tests and shipping them back.

Here are some actual kerfuffles that my students have encountered during their previous tests. (By the by – my spellcheck is fine with a singular kerfuffle, but it doesn't like plural kerfuffles? Go figure.)

- Many students have told me stories about their proctors screwing up the timing of each section. Some proctors cut the time short by mistake, while others added time to a section. The point of having a proctor is to ensure standardized testing conditions for every test taker in every location. So much for that.
- Another student reported back that his proctor was a little "loosey-goosey" with the timing. At the end of a section, the proctor said something to the effect of, "Oh, you're not done? Ok, you can take a few more minutes to finish the section." Oh no you can't! But these students could. Once again, way to take the "standard" out of standardized test.
- During the test, students can only work on one section at a time. They cannot go back to finish their work from a previous section, nor can they move ahead to start work on an upcoming section. However, a student recently told me she saw a nearby student working on the reading questions in section 1 while everyone was supposed to be working on the math questions in section 3. The proctor didn't catch it.
- Another proctor told my student he was done after section 3 instead of section 4! So my student left the test room, thinking he was done. Thankfully, the proctor realized this mistake rather quickly and ran into the parking lot to call him back in. Crisis averted, but jeesh. (And shame on my student; he had taken many practice tests, so he knew very well there were four sections and not three sections. Oh Ryan, you kill me.)
- And here's a personal favorite for paper test glitches: the 2021 April ACT got lost in the mail.

Yep. Really.

Hundreds of students took the April 17, 2021, ACT at a certain high school. Their answer sheets were sent back via FedEx. Those answer sheets got lost in the mail.

Yep. Really.

Now, those students were offered another opportunity to take the test (free of charge) or a full refund. But still... c'mon, man.

The digital test eliminates the potential for these sorts of errors!

- Timing is no longer the job of the proctor, so all students are guaranteed to have the same amount of time allotted for every section.
- The digital format only allows students to work on that specific section, without the chance to go forward or back to other sections.
- If a student is only done with three sections instead of all four, the digital test won't excuse the student early. (Still smacking my head on that one, Ryan.)
- The digital format eliminates the need for transporting the test to and from the testing location, so answer sheets can't get lost in transit.

So I'll agree with College Board on this one; the digital test format eliminates the potential for these types of mishaps. Plus, the digital test allows schools more flexibility as to when they can offer the exam, which also makes the test easier to give.

3 – More Secure

I'll agree on this point as well.

There have been many tales of bootleg tests winding up on the internet. This was especially true with the paper test overseas. The digital format makes the test much more secure.

Plus, the digital test only displays one question at a time on the screen. So, potential bootleggers can't photocopy an entire page of questions.

Also, because of the section-adaptive nature of the modules, cheating off your neighbors won't offer any advantage; they're not (necessarily) taking the same test that you are.

4 – More Relevant

College Board and the ACT folks try to make two cases for this.

First – they claim that the material on the test is more relevant in terms of what students see in school.

Second – they claim that the material on the test is more relevant in terms of the skills that students will need later in life.

My thoughts on the first point: nope.

My thoughts on the second point: are you flippin' kidding me?

On the first point – I won't bore you with my diatribes from the first few chapters. I'll just repeat my favorite refrain:

> **There is no perfect marriage between what you see in high school and what is fair game on the SAT and the ACT.**

Both tests include a significant amount of material that you've likely never seen before. See the Introduction and Chapter 1 for my full thoughts on this.

On the second point – oh please.

Are reading skills important? Of course. Are basic math skills helpful in life? For sure. Will it ever help you in life to know how the discriminant of a parabola affects the nature of its roots?

Never.

(But for a video that explains it – check it out here!)

https://tinyurl.com/DanFisch4

Here's a favorite meme I once saw on the interwebs. You may have seen it before:

> *"I'm so glad I learned about parallelograms instead of how to do my taxes. It really comes in handy during parallelogram season."*

This is a tad flippant, perhaps. Still, it makes the point nicely: most of what you learn in high school will be irrelevant the nanosecond that you finish high school.

I think it's Mark Twain who said:

> *"I have never let my schooling interfere with my education."*

I'm also reminded of a Paul Simon song lyric, where he jokes about the nonsense that he learned in high school. I'm with ya, Paul!

That's not meant to be pessimistic, but pragmatic. Unless you're entering very specialized fields of biology, you'll never need to know anything about the mitochondria of a cell. If you're not going to be a statistician, you'll never need to know about standard deviation.

Pay attention in school to do your best on your tests, midterms, comps, trimesters, finals, state regents, A.P. exams, I.B. exams, etc. *But do not believe it for a moment when the testing companies say that any of this crap is relevant beyond high school.*

My Real Beef with Each Test Company – And My Main Thesis of the Entire Book

In its practice test book, College Board repeatedly makes the point that the best way to prepare for the SAT is to "actively engage in challenging courses". They reiterate this claim throughout the book.

False. Utterly false.

The best prep for the SAT, and the ACT, is to learn what arbitrary topics are "fair game" on that test. If your high school classes don't cover those topics in the first place, it doesn't matter how actively you engage in them. You still haven't learned the topics that are fair game on that test.

I'll illustrate with the concept of margin of error, which has become increasingly popular on the SAT in recent years. A question on this topic might look like this.

Q. A Central Park intern stands at Columbus Circle, interviewing a random sample of people as they leave the park. She asks them how far they walked during their park stroll. She calculates that the estimated mean was 3.4 miles, with an associated margin of error of 0.3 miles. Which of the following is the most appropriate conclusion that can be drawn?

   A. It is likely that most visitors walked exactly 3.4 miles.
   B. It is not possible that any visitor walked less than 2 miles.
   C. It is likely that all visitors walked between 3.1 and 3.7 miles.
   D. It is plausible the mean distance walked for all visitors is between 3.1 and 3.7 miles.

I'll kick you into play, and then I'll let you answer. Margin of error measures... well... the margin of your error. Or put another way, it measures how much you're "off" by.

For example, if you measure something to be 85% with a margin of error of 2%, it means that your measurement might be 2% too high or 2% too low. So from 85, you can add 2 and subtract 2 to get the full range. This gives you a range of 83% to 87%.

But here's the thing: *that doesn't mean the answer is between 83 and 87. It means 83 to 87 is a plausible range for the mean.*

In other words, there could very well be values that are below 83 and above 87. Those numbers are not hard and fast boundaries. Again, it just means 83 to 87 is a plausible range for the mean.

Have my students learned that in school? Nope.

Does the SAT want them to know it? Yep.

Does knowing that concept have anything to do with "how challenging your coursework is"? Nope.

So, now that you understand how margin of error works, go back to the Central Park question. Take a moment and give it a shot. I'll be over here, wrestling with my Wordle.

(It's all about the vowel movement.)

If the mean is calculated to be 3.4, you would add and subtract the margin of error of 0.3. This gives you a range between 3.1 and 3.7. However, careful of choice C! It does *not* mean the final answer is between 3.1 and 3.7. Again, the magic words are that 3.1 to 3.7 is a *plausible range for the mean*. There very well could have been measurements outside of that range. The answer is D.

Now that you're warmed up, let's try another.

Q. Brian asks a random sample of amusement park visitors how long they had to wait for the flight simulator ride. He found that the mean wait time was 80 minutes, with a margin of error of 12 minutes. What is the best conclusion that can be drawn from Brian's survey?

  A. It is not possible that any visitors waited more than 92 minutes.
  B. It is not possible that any visitors waited less than 68 minutes.
  C. It is likely that all visitors waited between 68 and 92 minutes.
  D. It is plausible that the mean wait time for all visitors was between 68 and 92 minutes.

I'll be over here, finishing that Wordle. Give it a shot.

(Whew, I got it at the buzzer. My win streak is preserved.)

Many of my students are tempted by choice C. However, the answer is D. It is not enough to simply add the 12 and subtract the 12. We need those magical words: *plausible range for the mean.*

And this is a classic example of an arbitrary fact that the SAT wants you to know. Once you know it, it's not hard.

However, this concept is not taught in many math classes.

And it is certainly not relevant in life.

And it is *certainly* not dependent on how challenging your high school classes are.

So, College Board and the ACT can keep singing their song about how their tests are:

- measuring the knowledge and skills that are taught in schools.
- measuring the knowledge and skills that are relevant in life.

And as long as they do, I'll be over here singing "B.S." in reply.

(I really wanted to say it, but my editor and my mother told me not to.)

Only a small portion of SAT and ACT material overlaps with what my students see in high school. Period.

And even less of it is relevant beyond the classroom.

To say otherwise is simply untrue.

So Why Does College Board (or the ACT) Get to Decide What is "Most Relevant"?

Exactly.

This is the crux of standardized testing. There is nothing *standard* about it. Students from high schools A, B, and C might learn this math topic over there. Students from high schools X, Y, and Z might learn this grammar topic over there.

How can the SAT and the ACT perfectly align their tests with what all students have learned?

They can't.

We simply have to acknowledge that these test makers are the gatekeepers; they get to decide which topics are "fair game" and which topics are not. It's not fair. It's not right. It just is. And we have to deal with it.

In their materials, College Board talks about the surveys they conduct to decide what topics appear on the test and what topics get cut. And they're conducting more of these surveys over the coming years. But again, they get to decide. We just have to adapt.

For example, the paper SAT used to include a topic called *diction*. A grammar question would have said something like this:

I should of seen this trap coming.

The author doesn't mean to use the word "of" in that sentence. The sentence should say, "I should *have* seen that trap coming."

This is a topic that was tested on the paper SAT for many years. Then, College Board decided that diction would no longer be in play for the digital test.

I'm not calling that good. I'm not calling that bad. It just is. Diction used to be "fair game" on the test. Now it is not. **Because College Board says so.**

Ditto on the math section. For example, they announced that imaginary numbers would no longer appear on the digital SAT. I'm not saying that imaginary numbers are important. I'm not saying they're not. **But College Board gets to decide "we are cutting these topics over here and adding these topics over there".**

And likewise for the ACT, which is notorious for including random math topics. At the end of each math section, they love to throw in topics that have *never* appeared on the test before. They're not hard, per se. They're just *random*.

And these are the hoops that we must jump through. College Board is the vanguard of the SAT, just as the ACT folks get to decide what goes on the ACT. The best we can do is learn what is "fair game" on these tests, based on the practice materials they've released.

But to call it standardized is false.

To call it aligned with what students see in school is false.

To call it relevant to what students need to know beyond high school is false.

And to call it dependent on "taking challenging course work" is utterly false.

My Honest Thoughts on the Change

So, what are my honest thoughts on the shift from the paper SAT to the digital SAT? (Which is not to say that I haven't been honest up to this point!) To quote another tutor: *it's a bit of a nothing burger.*

Granted, there are aspects of the digital test that I think are an improvement, such as making the test more secure, the quicker turn-around time for the scores, etc.

But other changes are in the "who cares" category. For example, the grid-in answers can now be negative, the "no change" option was removed from the grammar questions, etc. *Nothing burgers indeed.*

So is it a "better test"? No.

My honest opinion: the SAT and the ACT are both incredibly useful and incredibly useless.

They are useful because they offer a standard yardstick against which all students can be measured. How can a student with a 4.1 GPA be compared to a student with an A+ average? And what about a student with a 103 average? As we said in the previous chapter, *everyone* now has a high GPA.

For example, when listening to a recent webinar for educators, I heard the tale of a student with a 4.3 GPA who was ranked 27th out of 125 in her class. With a 4.3, mind you. Which makes you wonder how off the charts the GPAs must be for students 1 – 26!

This gives you a sense of how high GPAs are a bit "diluted" now. A high average doesn't carry the same weight that it once did. So, these tests are designed to compare students using some standard barometer.

And I get that. Really. I do.

But this barometer is incredibly flawed.

Different students from different schools all learn different things! These tests only overlap so much with what students see in school.

Plus, there are the issues of equity and access that I discussed in Chapter 1. Again, that is why I created this book, along with my YouTube channel! (And speaking of topics that students don't see in school, here is a particularly nasty math topic that is new to many of my students. It's one of the harder topics, so check it out!)

https://tinyurl.com/DanFisch5

The bottom line: these tests don't reflect what you're learning in school, they don't indicate anything about your potential for future success, and they don't indicate anything about the quality of your character.

Are they relevant in life? Absolutely not.

But are they the necessary hoops to jump through? Yes.

And can I help you do well on them? You bet!

I'm reminded of Jimmy Fallon's line in the movie *Almost Famous:*

>"I didn't invent the rainy day. I just own the best umbrella."

That is how I feel about the SAT and the ACT. These tests are a crude assessment of arbitrary skills that are irrelevant the moment you finish the test. That said, I can help you do well on them!

So, let's put some *nothing burgers* on the grill and get to the good stuff: how to prepare for the test.

(Secret sauce coming in 3... 2... turn the page...)

Part II: Creating Your Customized Ten-Step Plan

"I was subjected to the LSAT three times and the SAT twice, unperforming in all five sittings. I was innately smart, but my mind was a wild stallion these standardized tests unsuccessfully tried to tame under time pressure. In response, I haphazardly kicked and bucked the tests' constraints, knocked down all paddock fences, until finally – and accidentally – I jumped over these artificial hurdles into school and my profession where I arrived.

Had Daniel been my tutor, I'd have taken each exam once, run each race full speed through to the finish line, and proceeded to the winner's circle.

My two children had the benefit of Daniel assisting them in their SAT prep. They stared straight into the intellectual heart of these counterintuitive exams together and fashioned a customized plan of attack.

Do what Daniel tells you to do."

— John G. Aicher, Jr. Esquire (Parent of Students in the Classes of 2013 and 2015)

In the first part of this book, we talked about what you can expect to see on the digital SAT and ACT. Now that you're more familiar with the formats of each test, let's map out a definitive step-by-step prep plan.

These are the same steps that I follow with my students! Here is the big picture of the steps we'll cover in the upcoming chapters.

Step 1:	Get a baseline for each test.
Step 2:	Decide which test you want to focus on.
Step 3:	Map out your timeline.
Step 4:	Start taking timed practice sections.
Step 5:	Start tracking your "cousin questions".
Step 6:	Start taking full timed practice tests.
Step 7:	Work on your cousin questions between practice tests.
Step 8:	Get ready for test week.
Step 9:	Work the TIR questions into your cousin bank.
Step 10:	Decide if it's time to retire.

Here we go.

Chapter 5: To SAT, or to ACT, That is the Question

"Daniel was really effective in capturing the areas I struggled in, and then used my strengths and weaknesses to choose the test that was the best fit for me. My PSAT numbers went from 1010 to 1220, and my SAT numbers went from 1270 to 1420."

— Alexander Billias (Class of 2022)

Deciding Which Test to Take

Sometimes, a student comes to me saying, "I heard that I should take the ACT because students do better on it." That depends! Some of my students are great candidates for the ACT. Others shouldn't touch it with a ten-foot pole.

Also, my students' parents sometimes ask me, "Do specific schools require one test over the other?" 10–15 years ago, the answer was yes. Likewise, colleges in certain regions used to have certain preferences. For example, the Midwest was big on the ACT, while schools in other locations preferred the SAT.

This is no longer the case; colleges will happily accept scores from either test now.

So the question becomes – which one should you take? Both tests have their own pros and cons. The first two steps will help you decide which test is the better fit for you.

Step 1: Get a Baseline for Each Test

To begin, you'll want to get baseline scores for both the SAT and the ACT. This means that you'll need to sit for a full SAT and a full ACT, timed and in one sitting.

I don't mean to take both tests back-to-back in one sitting. I'm not *that* mean. Do each test on a different day. But for each test, you'll want to do it timed and in one sitting.

There is a reason I'm being so strict about this. You're not just trying to get a sense of the scores; *you're trying to get a sense of the timing and the pacing*. This is especially critical for the ACT, where the timing is often the make-or-break factor. More on that in a bit.

If your school gives the digital PSAT, that will suffice! When my students take the PSAT in school, I don't ask them to do another baseline SAT on top of that. Keep in mind that the

PSAT scored is on a 1520-scale and not a 1600-scale. Even so, it is a reliable baseline for the SAT.

The same cannot be said about the pre-ACT. It is, frankly, far too easy. This goes for both the material and the timing. So if my students have done the pre-ACT in school, I don't completely discount it. Still, I ask them to sit for a full practice ACT before we begin.

Also, there's another reason I don't like the pre-ACT: it uses recycled questions! Many questions on the pre-ACT have appeared on previous ACT exams before.

And if you think that's wacky, here's a super fun nugget: the 2022 pre-ACT was a carbon copy of the 2018 pre-ACT. Yep. **They recycled the full test in its entirety.** (It's like in *Jaws 4*, where they literally used the same film footage from the original *Jaws* for when the shark falls into the abyss. The 2022 pre-ACT was the standardized test equivalent of *Jaws 4* pilfering its own franchise.)

So for many reasons, I'm not a fan of the pre-ACT. You'll want to sit for a full ACT instead.

And where should these baseline tests come from?

The key is to practice from *real* tests. That is to say, tests that are written by the actual test makers, and not tests that were written by a test prep company. This ensures the most authentic experience possible.

Here's where you can find them.

Finding SAT Practice Materials to Establish Your Baseline

At the time of this writing, College Board has four digital practice SAT tests available. (May they come out with more by the time you read this!)

But there is an interesting wrinkle with these four tests.

On their website, you'll find four PDFs in a section called "Full-Length Linear Practice Tests (Nonadaptive)".

You don't want those! Why not?

Notice the essential words there: *linear* and *nonadaptive*. These practice tests *do* include the same types of questions that appear on the digital exam. However, these practice tests are only offered in a PDF format. Therefore, they won't adapt as you take them. Everyone will see the same questions.

So don't use these tests from the website! Remember – the digital SAT is designed to be computer-adaptive. Your performance on the first module should dictate what you see on the second module. A paper test (or PDF test) can't do that.

The only students who should take these online PDF tests are those who are approved for paper test accommodations. Other students should download the College Board

Bluebook application. *That* is where you'll find digital practice tests. You can find this app at bluebook.app.collegeboard.org.

After you've downloaded the app, you can sign in with your College Board account. Once you're there, you'll see a bank of four practice tests as well. However, these four tests are not the same as those that are listed online. *The four tests on the Bluebook application are administered digitally.*

And those are the tests that you want! Why?

1. This ensures that you'll have the same digital experience as the real test (rather than taking the test on paper).
2. These tests reflect the computer-adaptive format. In other words, your performance on the first module will dictate what you'll see on the second module.

So for those paying attention, this means that there are not one, not two, but *three* versions of each SAT practice test! Huh? I'll use Practice Test # 1 to illustrate.

- The first version of Test # 1 is the nonadaptive PDF that College Board has listed on its website. Again, this is a nonadaptive linear version of the test.
- The second version of Test # 1 appears on the Bluebook app. By contrast, this test is adaptive! So if students do well enough on their first modules, they will be routed to the "high path"', or the harder questions in the second modules.
- The third version is the "low path" version of the test that appears on the Bluebook app. If students don't do as well on their first module, they will be routed to the easier questions in the second modules.

And likewise with Practice Tests # 2, 3, and 4. College Board offers the same three variations for each of these tests:

- The nonadaptive PDF on the website. Everyone will see the same tests here, regardless of their performance.
- The "high path" on the Bluebook app. If you do well enough on your first module, you'll be routed here.
- The "low path" on the Bluebook app. If you don't do as well on your first module, you'll be routed here.

And just a fun side note – certain questions overlap between these variations! For example, a question on the nonadaptive PDF Test # 3 also pops up on the Bluebook Test # 2. And within the Bluebook tests, some of the same questions appear on both the high and low paths.

So in case you encounter the same question on different practice tests, you're not crazy. It will occasionally happen.

Now, you can also find four practice tests in the College Board book: *The Official Digital SAT Study Guide*. However, you don't want to use them! Why? For the same reason that you don't want to take the practice tests that are offered in the online PDFs:

- These tests won't let you practice the digital format.
- These tests won't adapt as you take them.

College Board even reiterates this point throughout the book. They recommend that unless students are approved for paper test accommodations, they should take their practice tests on the Bluebook app.

I concur!

Still, for those who are curious, here's a breakdown of what tests appear in that book. Practice Tests # 1 and # 3 reflect the "low path" of the two Bluebook tests with the same numbers. Practice Tests # 2 and # 4 reflect the "high path" of the same two Bluebook tests. This way, students can get a glimpse into the full range of difficulty.

So, I'll play devil's advocate for a moment. The practice tests on the Bluebook app *do not* let you choose which path to take. These four tests in the College Board book do. So if you specifically want to practice the easier path, you can choose Practice Tests # 1 and # 3 in the book. If you want to see how you'll do on the higher path, you can choose Practice Tests # 2 and # 4 in the book.

Also, if you're approved for paper testing accommodations, then the practice book is fine.

But other than those two scenarios, I would skip the book and stick to the Bluebook app. That way, you create the authentic digital test experience, with sections that adapt based on your performance.

So in terms of planning for your baseline test, here's what I'd suggest.

If you've already taken a digital PSAT in school, that can serve as your baseline test. No need to do another. You can save the Bluebook tests for your practice rounds. But if you haven't taken the digital PSAT, you can take a Bluebook test for your baseline.

Or to save the four digital practice tests for later use, you can also take the PSAT that is listed on the Bluebook app! That test is adaptive as well. (So technically, there are actually five tests available on the Bluebook app – four SAT tests and one PSAT. Again, may College Board post more by the time you read this!)

All of the Bluebook tests have a built-in timer, which will ensure an accurate proctoring experience. When you sit for your baseline, be sure to do it timed and in one sitting. The test will score itself after you finish it.

Finding ACT Practice Materials to Establish Your Baseline

The ACT also publishes a book with real practice tests, called *The Official ACT Prep Guide*. Unlike the College Board practice book, this book is a good one to use! Why? Because you'll also be taking the ACT on paper. So the tests in the book reflect the same format you'll see on the real test.

To their credit, the ACT folks (usually) come out with a new practice book every year. At the time of this publication, the 2023 – 2024 edition is the most up to date one on the market. You can purchase it here:

https://tinyurl.com/DanFisch6

All of the tests in this book are pulled from actual tests from the past. You can pick any of them for your baseline test. The important part is to sit for it… you know what I'm about to say… *timed and in one sitting*. Why? Many students struggle with the timing factor on the ACT. And if you're one of them, that's ok! That's what you're trying to find out.

Use the following guidelines to self-proctor your baseline ACT test:

Section 1 English:	45 minutes
Section 2 Math:	60 minutes
Break:	5 minutes
Section 3 Reading:	35 minutes
Section 4 Science:	35 minutes

Some ground rules to self-proctor your baseline ACT:

- Create test day conditions as much as possible (phone off, computer away, etc.).
- Be strict with the timing constraints above! So if you run out of time on a section, you *must* move to the next section. Again, if you run out of time, you want to see by what margin.
- You can answer the questions within a section in any order, but you can only work on the questions *from that section*. No going forward to upcoming sections or back to previous sections.
- You can use a calculator in section 2, but not in section 4.
- You can skip the essay in section 5. You're welcome.

And then to score it:

- The book contains an answer key for each test, as well as a scoring guide.
- Tally how many questions you answered correctly in each section. (Once, a student did not deduct the number of questions she didn't have time for. You don't get points for those! So if you don't have time to answer 9 of the questions, be sure to subtract those questions, along with those you got wrong.)
- From there, there are scoring tables for each test. These tables will show you how to convert the number of correct answers to a final score for each section. It's a different curve for each test, so be sure to look up the table for that specific test.
- Your final ACT score, called your "composite" score, is made up of the average of all four sections. Add up the scores for each section and divide by 4. Then round that to the nearest whole number.

So if the average of all four sections comes out to a 25.25, your final score would be a 25. If the average comes out to a 25.5, your final score would be a 26, etc.

Once you have taken a baseline of each test, you can make a more informed decision about which test you want to focus on.

Step 2: Decide Which Test You Want to Focus On

There are many factors to help you decide which test to focus on; the scores are only one part of that equation. Still, let's start there.

The Scoring Factor

Certainly, you'll want to see how your scores compare between the two tests. This is where the concordance chart comes in.

The concordance chart is a table that allows you to see how SAT scores compare to ACT scores. This way, you can compare apples to apples. I won't include a table here because they tweak these numbers from time to time. Give it a web search. But just to give a few examples from the current concordance chart:

-An 18 on the ACT compares to SAT numbers in the 960 – 980 range.

-A 28 on the ACT compares to SAT numbers in the 1300 – 1320 range.

Again, these tables do change. And I'm sure they will again once students in the U.S. start taking the digital test! Check the current chart to see how your numbers compare.

Some of my students have very "lopsided" results. In other words, their scores from one test are far better than their scores from the other test. But other students have very comparable numbers between the tests.

So see how your numbers shake out. This will help you determine if you have a clear edge on one test vs. the other.

But putting the scores aside, there are many other factors to consider as well.

The Easy vs. Hard Factor

This is a bit of a generalization, but most of my students find that ACT questions are "easier". There are exceptions to this, of course. But if you discard the timing factor for a moment, I do agree that ACT questions are, for the most part, more straightforward than SAT questions.

Still, that doesn't necessarily mean to go with the ACT. Why? Because the timing factor on the ACT can be… well… brutal.

The Timing Factor

Timing is the main hurdle that steers many of my students away from the ACT. For example, on the ACT, you have:

- 45 minutes to answer 75 grammar questions. Plus, you have to read 5 passages!
- 35 minutes to answer 40 reading questions. Plus, you have to read 4 passages!
- 35 minutes to answer 40 science questions. Plus, you have to read 6 passages!

I often have students who only finish about 60-70% of each section within the time. And for others, it's closer to only 50%. If that's you, it might make your decision very easy to stick with the SAT. However, other students can finish the ACT questions within the time.

Simply put, the ACT is an "information regurgitation" test. It is a good fit for students who are good "information-extractors". Find a quick detail from the reading passage… and keep moving. Find a piece of data from a science table… and keep moving. Get in… get what you need… and get out. But keep moving!

I have many students who would be *great* candidates for the ACT if they had an extra 18 minutes per section. But given the timing constraints, they simply can't finish enough of the sections.

This is why you want to be so strict with your baseline ACT. It's not just to get a sense of the scores; it's to get a sense of the timing! If you don't have time for 3 or 4 questions, no big deal. But if you struggle to finish upwards of 20% or 30 % (or 40% or 50%) of an ACT section, that's another story. If so, the ACT might not be the right test for you.

The Digital Test vs. Paper Test Factor

And a big duh: each test is now given through a new format! The ACT is still given on paper (other than those trial digital tests we mentioned earlier). The digital SAT is now given on a computer. Students might favor one format over the other.

This is why it's so important to take your baseline SAT digitally (rather than through the PDFs I mentioned before). You're not just trying to get a sense of your scores; you're trying to get a sense of how you feel about the digital test "choreography". Maybe you like it. Maybe you hate it. But either way, see if you prefer one format over the other.

The Content Factor

On first glance, the SAT and ACT have many common components; both contain reading questions, math questions, and grammar questions. But within those sections, there are many differences.

Let's take a closer look at how the sections compare between the tests.

The grammar section on the paper SAT was very similar to the grammar section on the ACT. With the new digital SAT, things are considerably different.

Both tests will still include questions on punctuation, subject-verb agreement, misplaced modifiers, transitions, etc. However, the ACT still includes many questions on editing, organization, and shuffling sentences around. The digital SAT has cut those questions! Many new types of questions have taken their place. (See Chapter 12 for a full breakdown of what these newer questions are.)

Also, remember from Chapter 3, grammar questions on the digital SAT are all "clumped together". So you'll see all of the punctuation questions grouped together, followed by all of the transition questions grouped together, etc. This helps to avoid "context switching". You can have your "punctuation hat", followed by your "transition hat", etc. On the ACT, the grammar questions are all shuffled in together. So you might see a punctuation question, followed by an organization question, followed by an editing question, etc.

The reading questions on the tests are essentially testing the same skill: understanding what you read. Beyond that, though, there are many differences.

- ACT passages are longer. Each will then be followed by 10 questions.
- SAT passages are only one paragraph. Each will then be followed by only 1 question.
- And there are *many* new types of reading questions on the SAT. Again – check out Chapter 12 for a full breakdown!

But putting aside the questions themselves, *ACT reading questions are often much more straightforward.* Yes, there will be some tough ones in there. But ACT reading questions are often as simple as, "Which of the following things happened first chronologically?" They usually don't involve that much critical thinking; they just want you to find a certain detail. However, they do require you to move much more quickly.

Again, the ACT is all about "information extraction".

I'm going to skip math for a moment to talk about the ACT science section next. Why? *Because it's essentially another reading section!* The biggest misconception about the ACT science section is that it is testing "science". It is not. Most of these questions are not testing content-based science knowledge. So you don't need to study the atomic number of carbon or the steps for photosynthesis.

Instead, the science questions will ask you to analyze experiments, extrapolate data, and interpret charts and graphs. *It is essentially another reading section.* It just happens to be reading about scientific passages.

Now, of the 40 science questions, maybe 3 or 4 of them will require actual scientific knowledge. If they do, they'll usually ask for something very basic. For example, a content-based science question might want you to know that the charge of a proton is positive, or that an acid has a lower pH than a base.

This is a great video to cram for the knowledge-based questions that come up on the ACT science section!

https://tinyurl.com/DanFisch7

But for the most part, these questions are not quizzing you on scientific knowledge. They're more about scientific reasoning and data interpretation.

And then there is the math section. I saved this for last. The reason why – the ACT not only covers more advanced topics of math. *It covers more random topics of math.*

Say what you will about the SAT, but the math questions there are much more predictable. If you work through those practice tests, you'll see the same topics come up again and again (rules of a discriminant, systems of equations, etc.).

This is not the case for the ACT! The ACT does not have a finite list of topics that are considered "fair game". The first 45 out of 60 math questions, give or take, will cover the standard fare that appears on every test. But once you get to the last 15 questions or so, there is no guarantee of what topics you'll see. The ACT likes to throw in topics that have never appeared on the test before.

So it's not just that the math questions get harder as they move through a section. It's that the final few topics are so difficult to anticipate.

Now, depending on where you are in the scoring curve, this doesn't necessarily matter. For example, I recently worked with an ACT student who was starting in the mid-teens. Getting her up to the mid 20's was a huge jump! Her potential points were not coming from the last 15 questions; they were coming from the bread-and-butter topics that appeared in the first 40 questions. She didn't need to worry about those random topics at the end of the section. And she didn't have time for those questions anyway.

However, this is very relevant for students with math scores in the upper 20's who want to break the 30 mark. These students are earning their points on questions 1 – 45. Their remaining points are indeed coming from the final questions. However, those questions are a little "luck of the draw" in terms of what topics they'll see.

So, you might be well suited for SAT math if you are more comfortable with algebra 1 and a little geometry. But if you've seen more advanced topics (and if you can move through the sections more quickly), you could be a good candidate for the ACT.

Also, even though the ACT will pull from more advanced math topics, the question itself is often more straightforward. For example, an ACT math question might ask you to rewrite this logarithm: $\log_a b = c$

If you've seen logarithms before, this is not a hard logarithm question. It can be rewritten as $a^c = b$. However, many of my students have never seen this topic in school before. It's something you would see in a more advanced math class, but not in early algebra.

And this is the nature of many ACT math questions: *harder topics, but easier questions.* So if you've seen the topic before, the question itself is often not so bad. It just happens to be a more advanced topic.

And just a few other points of comparison between the math sections:

- You'll get to use a calculator on both the SAT and ACT.
- The SAT will give a reference table of formulas. The ACT will not.
- The SAT math has the 2 modules. The ACT math has 1 longer section.
- The SAT math will contain both multiple choice questions as well as student-produced response questions (where they won't list answers). The ACT math section will only contain multiple choice questions.

The How-Do-You-Feel Factor

Now, forget everything I just said. Forget the scores. Forget the timing. Forget that the ACT has a logarithm question while the SAT has a sentence completion question.

Just think about how you felt while taking each test.

Maybe you felt like the ACT reading questions were far more transparent. Or maybe you felt like the ACT science questions were total gibberish. Maybe you liked the shorter reading passages on the SAT. Or maybe you hated the digital SAT format.

You might have a very strong preference for one test over the other. Here's what a student recently texted me in reaction to her baseline ACT:

> *"Hi Daniel! I sat for the ACT this morning. I found it to be extremely stressful and upsetting. I honestly don't feel that the ACT is for me. The time constraints were really difficult for me, and the math section was exceptionally difficult because I had never seen most of it before."*

So, think about your gut reaction to each test, and add that to the soup as well! Your emotional reaction to the test is just as important as the actual numbers.

Should You Just Stick with the ACT While the Digital SAT Goes Through Its "Growing Pains"?

I have a feeling that many students will focus on the ACT in the coming year – not because it is necessarily the right fit for them – but because it is a "flight to the familiar".

I saw many students do this in 2016, when the 2400-scale SAT was replaced by the 1600-scale SAT. These students weren't necessarily better ACT candidates; they just didn't want to be the guinea pigs for the new SAT format.

And I understand this impulse. The new digital SAT might seem... well... new. But that doesn't mean to necessarily skip it! Be mindful of the factors above. *Especially the timing factor.* If you struggle to finish significant portions of the ACT, it's not necessarily a better choice.

What About Taking Both?

Some of my students do take both exams. I don't recommend this for everyone.

That said, if your scores are comparable between the tests, you might consider this. After all, there is a great deal of overlap between the material that you'll see on each test. For example, once you learn how to use a semicolon and a colon, you'll see those rules on both exams. (And for help on that topic, check out my lesson here!)

https://tinyurl.com/DanFisch8

If you decide to take both, my advice is to space them out by at least a month. That way, you can focus on *just* that format for the weeks leading into the exam.

What you should *not* do is alternate your practice tests. In other words, don't work on SAT sections one week, followed by ACT sections the next week. As you enter the month or two leading into a test, *only practice those types of questions.* This way, you can get used to:

- The timing and pacing for that specific test.
- The paper vs. digital format for that specific test.
- The types of questions for that specific test.
- The material that is relevant to that specific test.

Pick a train and stay on it for the stretch leading into the real test.

To Recap

- ACT questions are often "easier". Or at least many of them are more transparent.
- However, the timing of the ACT can be much more challenging. (Some students struggle to finish more than 60-70% of those sections within the timing constraints.)
- The ACT is still given on paper (see Chapter 2 for rare exceptions), while the SAT is given digitally.
- Verbal questions on the SAT are "clumped" together; this helps to avoid context switching. You can focus on one type of question at a time.

- SAT reading passages are just one paragraph, but the questions are often harder. ACT reading passages are longer, but the questions are often easier.
- The ACT includes a science section (which is not really testing "science"). The SAT will not.
- ACT math questions not only pull from *harder* topics; they pull from more *random* topics.
- While the ACT does pull from harder topics, the nature of the questions is often easier. So while the topic might be more advanced, it doesn't necessarily mean that the question is hard.
- Above all, the ACT is an "information regurgitation" test. It is a good fit for students who can extract data very quickly. The SAT might be a better match for students who need more time to process information.

So:

- Follow the steps above to get a baseline for each.
- Use the concordance chart to compare your scores! See if you have a clear edge on one vs. the other.
- And scores aside, think about how you *feel* about each test. Do you have a gut reaction either way?
- And if you decide to proceed with both, just make sure to space them out as much as you can. Have "tunnel-vision" on just that format for the weeks leading into your test.

Now you're ready to begin your...

...wait a second, aren't schools going test optional? Do you really need to be doing this?

Chapter 6: Wait a Second – Aren't Schools Going Test Optional Now?

"Daniel – you were great with (Child # 1), but we're going test optional for (Child # 2). See you in a few years for (Child # 3)."

— Many of My Clients

Hold up – do you even *need* SAT or ACT scores anymore? Since the pandemic, haven't many schools gotten rid of their testing requirements? Is any of this even necessary?

The short answer – it depends.

The better answer – read on!

What Exactly is "Test Optional"?

Let's start by defining what "'test optional" means. "Test optional" means that a college won't absolutely require you to submit your SAT or ACT scores; your application is complete with or without them. It's up to you to decide if you want to submit your scores.

This used to be more of a "black eye" on your application, as if you were hiding something. Since the pandemic, it's less of a red flag.

"Test free" (which was once called "test blind") means that colleges truly don't care about your test scores. They won't even look at your scores if you submit them.

And within that, there are many shades of gray, such as test flexible, test preferred, test neutral, etc. You may have heard these terms a bit more over the last few years.

The Evolution of These Policies

This did not start with the pandemic, though; test optional was around long before that. However, the pandemic *did* force many colleges to adopt a test optional policy, even if only a temporary one. Why? Because many students from the class of 2021 were simply unable to take the SAT or the ACT.

This started with the March 2020 SAT. Many students could not take this test because of last minute school closures. After that, the May and June SAT tests were canceled, along with the April 2020 ACT. Then, in the summer of 2020, certain testing sites did open up.

But these were few and far between. Many students traveled over state lines to take the test, only to find that their testing site was closed by the time they got there.

For example, many of my students who were signed up for the August 2020 SAT received this message from College Board right before their test:

> *Your test center has made the decision not to offer the August 29th SAT or has reduced its available capacity. Unfortunately, this means that your registration for the August SAT has been canceled.*

And there were many more last-minute cancellations into the fall of 2020.

Yeah, this was a fun time to be a tutor. (Insert sarcasm here.)

So, through no fault of their own, many students in the class of 2021 simply could not take either test. Other students did have the option to take the tests, but they didn't feel safe doing so during the height of the pandemic. By the time their applications were due, these students had no scores to submit. As a result, many colleges had to adjust their admissions criteria for the class of 2021.

Since then, different colleges have adopted a wide range of policies.

- Some colleges, like the Florida state school system, never stopped requiring test scores. Other colleges went back to requiring test scores within a year or two (like Georgetown, Purdue, and MIT).
- Others stayed somewhere "in the middle". They maintained a test optional policy, but they still encouraged students to submit their test scores.
- Others adopted a 1-year or 2-year test optional policy.
- Other colleges wanted to see how a policy change would affect a full cycle of students. These schools adopted a 4-year or 5-year test optional policy.
- Other schools decided to go test optional, but still awarded scholarships based on SAT or ACT scores.
- Other schools adopted a broader test optional policy, but still required test scores for specific programs within that school. For example, students who were applying to a certain nursing program or an honors college within the school might have still needed test scores, while applicants to other parts of the school did not.
- And other schools went fully "test free".

And so it continues to evolve today! It is a fluid situation; every school has its own policy across this spectrum.

So, track the admissions policies for any schools you're interested in. You might know from the start that you're only interested in schools that want test scores. Or you might know that you're looking at schools that don't. Or maybe you are looking at schools in the middle of the spectrum. Do your homework for the potential schools on your list; these policies are changing every day.

Test Optional "Doublespeak"?

There's also the ever-elusive question of how genuine colleges are when they say "optional". Many schools fly under a test optional banner, but then, their exact language varies. Some are very frank that when they say "optional", they mean it. And kudos to them! They're not saying "optional... wink wink", nor are they trying to play tricks with the language. They simply say, "If your scores are helpful, submit them. If they don't reflect your best abilities, don't."

But others use language that is more ambiguous. They say things like, "you will not be penalized for not submitting your scores...", but then they still emphasize that a good score is additive to your application.

So while they make the point that not submitting a score won't necessarily hurt you, they also make the point that submitting a good score can help you!

And this, understandably, can cause confusion.

To help you decide whether or not to submit your scores, you can look up the average scores for the schools on your list. From there, you can see how your numbers compare.

Still, bear in mind that good scores are relative; there are no guarantees.

In other words, it's never a situation where "scoring x and above means you're in" or "scoring y and below means you're out". Certain numbers just "put you in the conversation more". But there is no hard cut-off.

So don't be afraid to submit your scores if they fall under that range! Your test scores are *a component* of your application, but they are not *the component* of your application. Admissions offices take a holistic approach, looking at test scores, GPA, the rigor of your course work, extracurricular activities, letters of recommendation, work experience, essays, etc.

Plus, colleges will also consider how your scores compare to those from your school, as well as those from your geographic region.

So again, it's not a situation where 1340 and above guarantees admission, while 1330 and below guarantees rejection. There are many factors in play.

Full Transparency

All of that said, given that many schools are indeed test free now, I fully admit that you might not need to sit for the SAT or the ACT at all! I want to be fair about that point: not everyone needs to take these tests.

The relevance of standardized testing has waned since the spring of 2020. **Still, my philosophy is that it's better to have test scores and not need them than to need them and not have them.**

Now, I fully acknowledge that I say that as someone who runs a test prep company. I promise that I'm not saying that out of shameless self-promotion. I say it because of the factors I mentioned above.

Just to reiterate:

- Many schools never stopped their testing requirements.
- And many are returning to requiring test scores.
- Even test optional schools can require scores for certain programs within that school.
- There are various "shades of gray" within schools who fly under the test optional banner.
- And test scores can earn you scholarships or merit money!

Here are a few examples of that last point.

Potential $cholarships

Many of my students have earned scholarships or merit money because of their SAT and ACT scores. I've mentioned some of these examples in the testimonials throughout the book. Here are some highlights.

- One student qualified for a $240,000 National Recognition Scholarship from Fordham University. (See their full testimonial on the back cover!)
- Another student reported that his scores helped him qualify for a Presidential Scholarship, earning him $22,000 a year.
- One parent reported back that her daughter's test scores and GPA helped her qualify for $33,000 from Quinnipiac (Trustee Award), $27,000 from Connecticut College (1911 Scholarship), $38,000 from Loyola (Presidential Scholarship), $40,000 from URI, and $20,000 from Providence.
- I worked with a student who was starting with PSAT numbers in the 900's. We eventually got him up to a superscore of 1340! This helped him qualify for $29,000 a year from the Delaware Honors College program.
- And one student told me about The Bright Futures Scholarship in his home state of Florida. If students score above 1270, their tuition at a state school is 75%

covered. This is called the Academic Level Scholarship. If students score above 1340, their tuition is 100% covered! (Or more specifically, it was 1330 when he was a senior, but it has now gone up to 1340.) This is called the Medallion Level Scholarship. This student had scored 1030 on his November 2020 SAT. We got him up to 1340 on his August 2021 SAT! Putting aside those phenomenal score jumps, this was enough to qualify him for that higher scholarship.

So – optional schmoptional – your test scores can earn you some nice merit money!

The Bottom Line

Last year, the parent of one of my students showed me an email from her son's guidance counselor. The counselor had written the following:

> "It will not be a problem if he does not take the test. So many colleges are now test optional."

That is a blanket statement that is far too extreme. Parents, students, do your homework! Again, these policies are changing every day.

So I would vote to start the process in earnest. Begin your prep and see how things go. From there, let the numbers fall where they will. That will help you make a more informed decision.

Not to mention, the situation continues to evolve! Who knows what schools will return to requiring the tests in the coming years.

It is far better to have scores and not need them than to need them and not have them.

All of that said, yes, if you're only looking at schools with a guaranteed test free policy, you can skip these tests completely.

But if you're going to proceed, then on to step 3!

Chapter 7: Getting to Work – The Months Leading into the Test

"You do not rise to the level of your goals. You fall to the level of your systems."

— James Clear

Step 3: Map Out Your Timeline

Ok. You've taken your baseline tests. You have a better sense of whether you're aiming for the SAT or the ACT. You're now ready to begin your test prep! How do you now map out a timeline?

To answer this, we have to talk about the QAS and TIR reports.

The what?

The QAS and TIR reports are features that allow you to view your test questions after your scores come out. For the SAT, this is called the QAS report, or Question and Answer Services. For the ACT, it is called the TIR report, or Test Information Release.

These reports are an essential component of the test prep process because they offer students the chance to analyze countless aspects of their test taking performance, including:

- Every test question from that exam
- Where they made a careless error or a computation mistake
- Where they ran out of time within a section
- Where they ran out of steam at the end of the test
- What types of answer traps they fell for
- Any rules or topics they have yet to learn
- Where they haven't fully understood or memorized a topic they have learned

You can see how valuable these reports are! However, both companies are changing their policies on these reports. Let's start with the SAT and the QAS reports.

The SAT and the Disappearance of the QAS Reports?

The paper SAT was offered 7 times throughout the year: August, October, November, December, March, May, and June. However, only the October, March, and May exams offered the QAS reports!

So for years, it was essential to plan around those three specific months. If students were ahead of the curve, I would suggest that they sit for the October test. If they needed more time, I would strongly recommend the March and May tests. It was all about timing the season for the QAS reports.

However, you'll notice I've been using the past tense. At the time of this writing, the QAS reports seem to be going away. It looks like the digital SAT will no longer offer students the chance to view their questions after they take the test.

And boy I hope I'm wrong about that.

Now, we are learning more about the digital tests every day. Hopefully, the day after this book gets published, College Board will announce that the digital tests will indeed offer the QAS reports. We'll see!

Follow my website for any updates: www.fasttracktutoringllc.com. I'll keep you posted as things evolve.

But if the QAS reports are truly a thing of the past, then you no longer need to plan your timeline around them.

Thankfully, the TIR reports *are* still available for the ACT! Still, the schedule there is changing as well.

The ACT and a Shift in the TIR Schedule

Just like the (retired) paper SAT, the current ACT is offered 7 times a year: September, October, December, February, April, June, and July. For years, the TIR reports were offered in December, April, and June. However, for the 2023 – 2024 academic year, the TIR reports will now be offered in *September*, April, and June.

Why are they changing that first month? I don't know. Will it stay that way for academic years that follow, or will they go back to the December, April, and June rotation? I don't know.

That said, let's assume that this new schedule is going to be the new norm. If so, here's what I'd suggest.

Notice the gap in the timing: after the September exam, the TIR report is not offered again until the April exam! You can still take the ACT in October, December, and February, but those months won't offer you a chance to analyze your test questions.

So Plan A would be to sit for the ACT during September of your junior year. Full disclosure, that might be too soon for many students. But students who feel prepared (or even for those who are saying "what the hell, why not?") can take a shot at the September ACT. This lets them analyze the questions from their TIR reports before their upcoming October, December, and February tests.

Or Plan B would be to settle into junior year, learn more material, and fully prep over the winter for the April and June exams. Those are the other two months that offer the TIR reports.

Now, there are some exceptions to that. For example, students who take the Sunday exam only have access to their TIR reports in April. Also, students with time accommodations don't always get access to their TIR reports. And there are some other exceptions as well. But for the majority of students, the TIR reports are offered for those dates: September, April, and June.

That doesn't mean that you shouldn't take the ACT during the other months. Just keep in mind that those other months, at least according to the current ACT calendar, won't offer the TIR reports. The September, April, and June exams will.

It's all about timing the season so that you can analyze your questions!

Here's how the timing goes for getting the TIR reports back.

ACT scores typically start to appear online about 10 days after the test. This is not a guarantee, but the scores usually appear two Tuesdays after the exam. Then, within a few weeks, the TIR reports will appear online as well. There is no set timeline of when; it varies from student to student.

But just for context, here's when the TIR reports came out for some recent test dates:

- My students who took the December 2022 exam were able to see their TIR reports starting around January 10th.
- My students who took the April 2023 exam were able to see their TIR reports starting around May 9th.
- My students who took the June 2023 exam were able to see their TIR reports starting around June 21st.
- My students who took the September 2023 exam were able to see their TIR reports around September 25th.

Again, I say "around" because these dates vary from student to student. Some students have to wait longer. But this gives you a sense of the timeline. It's not a guarantee, but you'll usually get to analyze your questions before the next test date comes around.

(Side note – there is an extra fee to add the TIR report to your registration, but it is worth every penny.)

Back to Step 3

So, at the time of this writing:

- It looks like the QAS reports for the SAT are going away. (Angrily shakes fist at the sky.)
- It looks like the TIR reports for the ACT are shifting to September, April, and June. (Quizzically looks at the sky?)
- Will the QAS reports come back? I hope so.
- Will the TIR reports stay on this new rotation for the years to follow? I don't know.

Let's assume that the answer to the first question is no (grrrrrr). Let's assume that the answer to the second question is yes (shrug).

With those assumptions, let's proceed.

Step 4: Start Taking Timed Practice Sections

You can start slow. Start by familiarizing yourself with the directions for each section, as well as the format for each question. (Be sure to check out Chapters 12 and 13, where I cover every type of question you'll see!)

Once you're familiar with the format and the directions, you can start taking timed practice sections. For the SAT, you can use the Bluebook app. For the ACT, you can use the book that I mentioned in Chapter 5.

Ease into it at first. Maybe do a timed verbal section one day, followed by timed math section a few days later. Space them out between your schoolwork as needed.

As you take these sections, you'll likely come across material that you've never seen before. (Have I mentioned yet that these tests don't align with what you see in school?)

So take notes on any new topics you encounter! Maybe you've never seen a box and whisker plot before. Or maybe you've never learned the difference between when to use a comma vs. a semicolon. Check out my lessons here for help on each of those topics!

Here is the video that includes my lesson on box and whisker plots. (Side note – until recently, this topic had only appeared on the SAT. But over the last year, it has popped up on a few ACTs as well!)

https://tinyurl.com/DanFisch9

And here is the video that includes my lesson on commas and semicolons. This topic is quite popular on both tests.

https://tinyurl.com/DanFisch10

Whenever you come across an unfamiliar topic, jot it down.

I'll give both companies credit on this point. The ACT book has some very helpful explanations. Likewise, the Bluebook app will guide you to detailed explanations after you finish your practice sections.

And of course, check out my videos to review any topic where you need more help!

You can also make flashcards. Write any rule, formula, term, title, or prompt on the front of the card. Then on the back of the card, you can write the corresponding explanation or answer.

I'll use the two topics above for a quick example. On the front of a flashcard, you can write something like, "What does the middle of a box and whisker plot mean?" On the back of the card, you would write, "the median".

Ditto for that grammar rule. On the front of the flashcard, you can write, "When to use a semicolon". On the back of the card, you would write, "between two full thoughts".

(These rules have other moving parts as well; check out the links above for a deeper dive into these topics!)

Now, studying the rules is important, of course. But test prep is about more than just rote memorization. It's about recognizing how the same topics appear again and again.

And that leads us to the most important aspect of test prep: *brand recognition of the question.*

Let's see what I mean.

Step 5: Start Tracking Your "Cousin Questions"

What are cousin questions? I'll get there shortly.

After years of working with students, I have learned one crucial thing: the best test takers are by no means the smartest students. They are those who can identify the underlying principle of a question.

The SAT and ACT constantly repeat the same "brands" of questions. The questions themselves might change from test to test, but the underlying concept remains the same.

Let's look at a grammar example. I'll give away that something is wrong with the underlined portion of this next sentence.

> Brought over from Polynesia hundreds of years ago, <u>Australia now incorporates the bird as a mascot</u>.

Why is that sentence incorrect? Feel free to read it again. I'll be over here, seeing if Costco still carries my favorite cracker.

(They don't. Darn.)

So what's the error in the sentence above? I'll reread the introduction: "Brought over from Polynesia hundreds of years ago…."

What noun in that sentence was brought over from Polynesia hundreds of years ago? The bird.

According to the rules of grammar, an introductory phrase must be followed by the noun that it describes. In other words, the introduction of this sentence is describing the bird. **That means "the bird" must come right after the introduction.** The sentence should say, "Brought over from Polynesia hundreds of years ago, **the bird** is now incorporated as the mascot of Australia."

The way it's written, what does it sound like? The word "Australia" comes after the introduction. It sounds like *Australia* was brought over from Polynesia. Like… they picked up Australia and moved it across the ocean.

This is a very popular rule on both the SAT and the ACT. So one more time: ***an introductory phrase must be followed by the noun that it describes.***

Now that you've seen the rule, let's try another question that's doing the same thing. Think about the error in the underlined portion of this sentence.

Opened to the public in 1886, <u>tourists make The Statue of Liberty one of the most visited landmarks in New York City</u>.

I'll give you a second. Read it again and give it a think.

(But they do have my organic turkey! Score.)

Once again, we have to think about what noun the introduction is describing. What noun was "opened to the public in 1886"? The Statue of Liberty! That *must* come after the introduction. The sentence should read: "Opened to the public in 1886, *The Statue of Liberty* is one of the... blah blah blah."

The rest doesn't matter. As long as T*he Statue of Liberty* comes next. That's the noun that was opened to the public.

The way that the sentence is written, what does it sound like? It sounds like *tourists* were opened to the public in 1886.

You probably found that second example much easier than the first. Why? *Because you learned to spot the underlying mechanism of the question.* The fancy name for this is a "misplaced modifier", but who cares! As long as you can recognize, "Oh... they're doing that thing where the intro has to be followed by the subject."

And this is what I mean by *brand recognition*. My best students can look at that Statue of Liberty question and say, "That's an Australia Bird question."

YES!!!!

It's all about training your brain to recognize the underlying concept of the question.

And I refer to questions like these as **cousin questions**. Even though the specifics have changed, the concept is identical.

Let's see how this applies to a math concept.

> Melissa's balloon floats at a certain distance off the ground. However, it loses enough helium so that it falls by a constant amount each day. If the following equation can be used to model its height h in feet:
>
> $$h = -.75x + 15$$

What does the .75 represent?

What does the 15 represent?

I'll give you a minute. I'll be here, finalizing my shopping cart.

(Coconut Keto Clusters?? Impulse buy, oh fine.)

You might have recognized that this is the equation of a line: $y = mx + b$. In the equation of a line, m represents the slope and b represents the y-intercept.

But let's go a bit further than that. What do those terms mean in a real-life situation? The slope represents the rate of change, and the y-intercept represents where you start. So in the case of the balloon, the .75 indicates the rate of change. For every unit of time, the balloon is falling .75 feet. The 15 represents the starting height. In other words, it starts 15 feet off the ground.

This is a very popular brand of question as well. The test loves to use the equation of a line to represent a real-world scenario. When they do, the slope is the rate of change, and the y-intercept is where you start.

So let's see how this same concept comes up on a cousin question.

> Elliott opens a savings account. He keeps it open for q months. If the total amount d can be modeled by the equation:
>
> $$d = 40q + 300$$

What does the 40 represent?

What does the 300 represent?

I'll give you a minute. Give it a shot.

(And don't even get me started on their almond butter. Perfection.)

Just like the last question, the 40 is slope, or the rate of change. So in this case, it represents how much money Elliott is putting into the savings account each month. The 300 is the y-intercept, or the starting amount. In this case, it means he started with an initial deposit of 300.

You probably found that second example easier than the first. Why? You are no smarter than you were six minutes ago, nor is the question any easier. What changed? *You learned to recognize the brand of question being tested.*

And so it is with every question on the test!

You will never see any of these questions ever again. Ever. However, you will see that *brand* of question again. On every. Single. Test.

The test loves to represent a real-world scenario with the equation of a line. I have my students call this concept "Melissa's Balloon". The test also loves to test misplaced modifiers. I have my students call those questions "Australia's Bird".

And this is what we do with every type of question!

We come up with a silly little name for every type of question. I don't use these titles just to be silly. I use them so that my students can start to recognize how these questions are all identical.

And it works!

When my students walk out of their real exams, they often text me something like "I saw an Australia Bird question!" Or they'll say something like, "There were 2 questions dealing with Melissa's Balloon!"

And this is, literally, the best thing my students can say. They're not saying that the test "felt easy". Instead, what they're really saying is that they truly recognized the underlying principle of the question.

And that is the main goal of test prep: **pattern recognition**. It's all about looking at a question and being able to say, "They're showing me A... so it's time to do B." Again, you'll never see any of these questions ever again. But you will see that *brand* of question again.

On every. Single. Test.

Here is what a recent student said about our process of identifying cousin questions:

> *"Daniel and I worked together for several months, and the work we did really helped get my scores up. For example, he would give 'code names' to specific math rules to help me spot them. After reading a question, I could tie it back to a concept we had seen. This really helped me become a better test taker!"*

Exactly! This student was able to improve his PSAT scores from 950 to 1180. He then improved his SAT scores from 1190 on the December 2021 exam to 1310 on the October 2022 exam.

This process works! It's all about brand recognition of the question.

(And just to reiterate my rant from Chapter 4 – it has nothing to do with "taking challenging classes". It has to do with learning what arbitrary topics the test wants you to know.)

So let's talk about how you can start to incorporate this into your test prep.

- As you take practice sections, start to look for what "brands" of questions you're missing.
- Then, in a notebook, keep a full page for each topic.
- On that page, keep a running list of any cousin questions that popped up for that topic.

For example, maybe you keep missing grammar questions that are dealing with colons. You can create a page titled "Colons". On that page, you would write down every question where you missed that topic. So you might jot down something like, "SAT Test 2 – Module 1 – Question 23", or "ACT Test 3 – Question 63".

Likewise for math. Maybe you keep missing systems of equations. It gets its own page! Title each page with the name of the topic you're missing. Then fill in those pages with the corresponding questions you miss. The more practice sections you do, the more cousin questions you'll add to your question banks!

And now the real magic starts: working on your cousin questions in tandem with full length practice tests.

And just a side note, here are my lessons for the topics I just mentioned.

For more practice with "Australia's Bird" and misplaced modifiers, go to the video here! You'll see that same question, along with some harder variations.

https://tinyurl.com/DanFisch11

For more practice with modeling a situation and Melissa's Balloon, here ya go!

https://tinyurl.com/DanFisch12

For my lesson on colons, check out this guy.

https://tinyurl.com/DanFisch13

And systems of equations are literally the most popular topic on the test – so it's definitely worth a watch here.

https://tinyurl.com/DanFisch14

And keep hitting other videos to help with other topics!

Step 6: Start Taking Full Timed Practice Tests

As you get closer to your real exam, you'll want to graduate from timed sections into full practice tests. You can start to sprinkle these in as early as you want. At the latest, start taking full tests about 4-6 weeks before your actual test. Space them out as needed between rounds of heavier schoolwork.

And as I mentioned a few chapters ago, you want to create authentic testing conditions. So, for any practice tests:

- Create an environment without any distractions (phone off, computer away, etc.).
- You can answer the questions within a section in any order, but you can only work on the questions *from that section*. No going forward, and no going back.
- When the time is up on a section, you *must* move to the next section.
- For the ACT, use the bubble sheet to transfer your answers.
- Sit for the practice tests on weekends, not after school.
- If you can, try to take them during the same morning window when you'll take the real test.
- Don't cheat on your practice tests. (Do I really need to say this?? Evidently, I do. Over the years, I've caught several students cheating on their practice tests. Because... you know... that helps you improve your score for the future. If you're getting something wrong, *tell your tutor that!!* That is helpful information. End of PSA, thank you.)
- And after you score your practice test, add any topics that you missed to your cousin question banks!

So did you miss another system of equations? Add it to your page where you're gathering those types of questions. Or did you miss a new grammar topic this round? Create a new page for it! The more practice tests you do, the more topics you'll "catch in your net", so to speak.

Which brings us to the next step: working on your cousin questions between your practice tests.

Step 7: Work on Your Cousin Questions Between Practice Tests

Full practice tests will monopolize a lot of your time. If you know that you're coming into a particularly busy week of school, you can lighten the load as needed.

So, during any heavier stretches of schoolwork:

- Study your rules and formulas.
- Watch any videos that pertain to those rules!
- Take independent sections instead of full tests.
- And work on your cousin questions!

The cousin questions are a fantastic way to utilize your shorter windows of downtime. Think of them as "spackle" for your schedule; you can work on them during a 27-minute stretch over here, or a 33-minute stretch over there, etc.

This way, you won't overload your schedule during a heavier stretch of schoolwork.

Also, this gives you targeted practice on a specific type of question! So let's say that you're still struggling with systems of equations. By working on four or five of these questions consecutively, you'll start to see the common thread between them. Likewise with Melissa's Balloon, Australia's Bird, or any other topics that you find. It's all about pattern recognition.

And this is where the cousin questions really work their magic. By working on your cousin questions consecutively, you train your brain to recognize how all of these questions are the same.

(And of course, watch the corresponding videos for more help as needed!)

Feel free to get creative with the titles that you use for each topic. You've already seen some of my silly little mnemonic devices, like "Melissa's Balloon" for linear growth and "Australia's Bird" for misplaced modifiers. My students know these titles very well.

And you can do the same thing! You can name a certain topic after your Uncle Arty, a certain sports team, or one of your favorite types of food. Whatever works for you. Use a title that helps you recognize the underlying mechanism of the question.

As you enter the month leading into the test, plan for at least two full length practice tests (always on weekends). Fill the time in between with studying, watching my videos, independent sections, and reviewing your cousin questions.

Working on cousin questions consecutively helps with that most essential aspect of test prep: **pattern recognition**. "They're showing me A… so it's time to do B." The cousin questions are designed to help you recognize how all of these questions are the same.

Because they are!

The Cram Plan

Now I know what some of you are saying. "Daniel, the plan above sounds great… for someone who planned ahead. But I'm only reading this (insert incredibly short timeframe here) before my test."

I understand.

I sometimes get these calls from new students as well. Just this past spring, I got an email from a parent asking me, "Can you meet with my daughter six times in the next two weeks before her May SAT??"

And perhaps you are in a similar time crunch now.

Is it ideal? No. Can you still make progress? Yes!

Let's assume that you're looking at a runway of less than two weeks from the test. Given that you're going to be on the express plan, I'll go with bullet points instead of prose here.

- Go read Chapters 11 – 13 as soon as you finish this! This way, you can familiarize yourself with the types of questions you'll see, my "quick-fire tips", and the most essential test taking strategies.
- Ideally, sit for a full test, timed and in one sitting.
- Or at the very least, sit for piecemeal sections. But do each section timed.
- Score the test (or those piecemeal sections).
- See if there are any topics that you missed more than once. For example, did you really struggle in that stretch of five or six punctuation questions? Or did you miss all three questions that dealt with systems of equations? See where your "repeat offenders" are.
- Assuming that you don't have time to sit for another full test, leaf through other practice sections to pull more "cousin questions" for those topics! So instead of monopolizing your time with a full grammar section, work on another batch of punctuation questions. Or instead of sitting for another full math section, plow through as many systems of equations as you can find.
- And hit my videos that pertain to any topics where you need help!

But by doing this:

- You'll still familiarize yourself with the instructions for each section, as well as the format of each question.
- You'll still get a sense of your timing and pacing within each section.
- You'll be able to pinpoint some "repeat offenders" to work on the topics that you're missing the most.

Is it the full battery? No. Is it better than nothing? Definitely!

"As parents, we all want our children to do well in life, and we try to give them every advantage to succeed. When it came time to prepare for college, I began the search for a tutor who could bring out the best in our daughter and focus on the academic skills she would need to be accepted to an excellent college. I had heard about Dan Fischer through the grapevine, and almost everyone said that he was impossible to get because he was in such demand. I called Dan anyway, and – lucky for us – he had a slot for our daughter!

Dan possesses superior knowledge about the SAT and ACT exams. He believed in my daughter, pushed her when needed, and gave her truthful pokes in the right direction. There is no doubt in my mind that Dan helped our daughter get into the college of her choice.

Dan is very serious about what he does, and he is totally committed to helping students achieve their goals. I don't see anyone being more knowledgeable about this arena than Dan. Follow his guidance; you won't be disappointed. Do it!"

— Lisa Zindman (Mother of a Student in the Class of 2018)

Chapter 8: The Week Leading into the Test

"Daniel's methods for SAT and ACT preparation were organized, thorough, and practical. After my daughter finished her final session with Daniel, she turned to me and said, 'Well, Daniel gave me everything I need to do well on the test.' You really can't ask for more than that!"

— Erin's Mom (Parent of a Student in the Class of 2020)

Step 8: Get Ready for Test Week

You've arrived! You are officially approaching game day (or insert non-sports metaphor here for those who don't care about the volleyball). Here are some checklists as you enter the home stretch. (Oops, I went back to a sports metaphor. Sorry.)

And suffice it to say – all of the tips in this chapter are relevant for both the SAT and the ACT, except those that deal with getting your testing device ready. Those tips only apply to the digital SAT.

The Week of the Test

- Study any rules, formulas, or shaky topics that are still giving you trouble. You're allowed to miss a question because of its difficulty, because of the timing factor, or even because of a careless error. Make sure you don't miss any questions just because you can't remember a certain math formula or grammar rule.
- Review any cousin questions as needed.
- And review any of my videos that correspond to those topics as needed.
- Look up the route to your test center if it's unfamiliar.

(Side note – once, a student thought he was taking the test in Farmingdale, New York. So he headed to that high school. Turns out, he had indeed signed up for Farmingdale... *but Farmingdale, New Jersey*. As such, he couldn't take the test when he showed up to the New York location.)

(Yes, that story is true.)

- Wake up at the same time that you will for the test.

That is especially important if you're taking the test over a school break or summer recess. Resist the temptation to sleep in during the days leading into the test. Give your body a few days to adjust to the early wake-up time.

Getting Your Testing Device Ready

- For those taking the SAT, download the Bluebook app on your testing device. (Hopefully, you've been practicing sections from there already!) This might require you to update your operating system.

    You can find it here: bluebook.app.collegeboard.org.

- One to five days before the test, you'll have to log on the app, agree to the terms and conditions, and complete the exam setup. This will give you access to your admissions ticket.
- You can bring a mouse, but you cannot use multiple screens. See the College Board page for other restrictions.

Borrowing a Device

- If you need to borrow a testing device, you'll need to submit a request at least thirty days before the exam.

    You can find more info at satsuite.collegeboard.org/digital/device-lending.

- Submitting a request does not guarantee access to a device, so be sure to do so early in case you need to make other accommodations.
- If you're taking the test on a school-managed device, make sure that the Bluebook app is loaded there.

The Night Before the Test

- Do a final review of any rules, formulas, notes, and flashcards.
- Put aside all testing materials (ID, admission ticket, pencils for scratchwork, calculator, snacks, water, etc.).
- Speaking of your calculator, make sure it has fresh batteries. (I have too many stories about students whose calculator died during the test.) For a list of approved calculators, go to sat.org/calculator.
- Make sure your computer is fully juiced for a three-hour charge. You can bring a power cord, but there is no guarantee that you'll have access to an outlet. A portable charger is a good idea too. (This is especially important if you have extended time.)
- Put aside comfy clothes for both a hot and a cold room. For example, have both a t-shirt and a hoodie ready to go.
- You can bring snacks and a drink, but they must be stored under your desk during the test.

- You can also bring paper to use for scratch work on the digital exam.
- Relax, do something fun, and get a good night's rest.

  Seriously. Do something fun and chill. Don't stay up until 2 am doing practice sections. Ease off the gas and relax. Watch a movie. Play a board game. Take your mind off everything, have a little fun (but not too much), and go to bed.

- And do I need to tell you to set your alarm? Evidently, I do. I have too many stories of students not waking up in time for the test. Don't be that student.

The Morning of the Test

- Eat a good breakfast.
- Read something (newspaper article, something online, etc.).
- Get in 10-15 minutes of light cardio exercise.

The key is to wake up both the brain and the body. Don't roll out of bed and show up to the test totally cold. ***Think of the test like an athletic event.*** Seriously. Get your circulation going so you can sustain your energy throughout the exam.

Potential Proctoring Problems

Unfortunately, my students have told me about many funky tales from their test room. I included some in Chapter 4. Here are a few of my favorite nuggets.

- Proctors were talking to other teachers at full volume during the exam.
- A proctor fell asleep, and the snoring distracted my student.
- A proctor wrote the wrong ending time for the section. (The digital SAT should alleviate this problem, but it's still a possibility for the ACT.)
- The fire alarm went off, so students had to leave in the middle of a section. And when they came back, the proctor did not give them that time back!
- And many other fun stories as well (a student needing to leave because of a bloody nose, another student trying to cheat off one of my students, etc.).

You should be fine. These anecdotes are few and far between.

Having said that...

Test Room Tips

- Be your own advocate in the test room! If something goes wrong, say something. Tell the kid at the adjacent desk to leave you alone. Tell the chatty proctor to quiet down. And certainly, correct them if they write the wrong time on the board.

  Again, the digital format will alleviate many of these issues. Still, don't be afraid to speak up if something goes wrong.

- Leave your laptop open on the breaks.
- Make sure to move around on the breaks. Even if you don't have to use the restroom, get up and leave the room. Get the blood flowing, regain your energy, and get out of the headspace of the room.
- Utilize the breaks to have your snacks and drinks.
- Remember what we said earlier in the book – don't cheat! You are not (necessarily) taking the same test as the students sitting near you. Focus on your own test and don't worry about anyone else. (Plus, you know, the whole morality thing.)

A Note on the Experimental Questions

- Remember – the SAT will sprinkle in a few questions that don't count towards your score. However, you won't know which questions are experimental and which are "operational". So just treat every question like it counts.
- And if there's a question you hate, cross your fingers; it might not count towards your score! Just put your best guess and move on to the next.
- The ACT will slip in an experimental section 5... sometimes. Just like the SAT experimental sections from the paper test, the ACT experimental section does not count towards your score. The ACT folks are testing questions for the future.

But I say sometimes because occasionally, my students are excused without having to sit for this section! But if you are forced to sit for it, don't stress over these questions.

Other Things to Remember

- While taking the SAT, *don't think about the adaptive sections!* More specifically, don't go down the rabbit hole of saying, "Wow, these questions seem far too easy... I guess I didn't make the cutoff for the harder module... looks like I'm screwed." There are easy questions in both module paths! And it's nothing you can control in the moment anyway. Do your best on whatever questions you see.
- On the digital SAT, you can flag questions that you'd like to return to. When you reach the end of a module, use any remaining time to work on these questions.
- And on both tests, no matter what, make sure to answer every question!
- Above all, remember this: *there will be no surprises*. If you've been taking full length practice tests, you'll be very familiar with the "greatest hits" of each test. You're going to see questions such as "Melissa's Balloon", "Australia's Bird", etc.

I'm not saying don't be nervous. That's natural. Be nervous! But once you start taking the test, notice how many of your "friends" start to appear on a question. Australia's Bird over there! Trinomial factoring over there! You'll start to spot many "cousins" of topics that you've seen before. Let that familiarity carry you through each section.

Whew, you made it! Good job. After the test, go do something fun. Have a nice big lunch. Take a nap. Ride a bike. Zone out with a video game. But don't stress over it anymore. You've been through a lot!

Step 9: Work the TIR Questions into Your Cousin Bank!

Now you get to wait for your scores to come out. How long does that take?

Students who took the paper SAT would typically see their scores 13 days after they took the exam. This was not a guarantee, but usually, the scores would be posted two Fridays after the exam.

College Board says that the digital test will shorten that timeline to "a matter of days".

That would be great!

That said, I had students outside of the United States take the digital SAT in the spring, summer, and fall of 2023. Those scores still took 13 days to appear online.

Granted, these were the very first digital tests to be given. So it's certainly possible College Board will improve its systems and shorten this timeline moving forward. We shall see!

ACT scores get posted about 10 days after the test. So if the test is given on a Saturday, the scores usually come out two Tuesdays later. That's not a guarantee, and there are students who have to wait longer. But that's usually the schedule. It's not based on alphabetical order or geographic region. It's just luck of the draw.

And just to get *really* into the weeds – when do the scores come out on score release day? It also depends. My students usually are able to see their scores "in waves". Many can see their scores by the time they wake up. Then another batch can view their scores between 10 am and 11 am. Others have to wait until later in the day.

And beyond that, some have to wait several days, and others might even have to wait several weeks. Don't be alarmed; it's less frequent, but it happens.

Now, hopefully, you hit your target scores sooner than later. But if you need to take the ACT test again, take advantage of those months that offer TIR reports!

The TIR reports *usually* come out before the next test date. I'd mentioned some recent dates back in Chapter 7. Just to recap:

- My students who took the December 2022 exam were able to see their TIR reports starting around January 10th.
- My students who took the April 2023 exam were able to see their TIR reports starting around May 9th.

- My students who took the June 2023 exam were able to see their TIR reports starting around June 21st.
- My students who took the September 2023 exam were able to see their TIR reports around September 25th.

Again, I say "around" because these dates vary from student to student. It's not a guarantee. Sometimes, the TIR reports are delayed. So yes, it's possible that you may not be able to view your test questions before the next round. But usually, you will!

When the TIR report gets posted online, you'll be able to view the full PDF of your test. You'll also be able to view the answer guide that lists the correct answers, along with what you put for each question.

This is gold, Jerry! GOLD!!! (Yes, that's a Kenny Bania reference, for those who were watching NBC in the 90's.)

Add these questions to your cousin question banks. There will probably be some overlap with some topics that you've seen before. But if you come across a new topic, add another page! (That can definitely happen for those last few ACT math questions where they throw in those *random* topics.)

From there, work those questions into your practice rotation.

Unless you're done! But how do you know if you are?

"Both of my daughters were extremely fortunate to have had Daniel as their SAT and ACT tutor. They would never have done so well on their exams without Daniel's expertise and extensive knowledge.

It is so amazing that he is sharing all of his knowledge, expertise, and coveted insider tips in his book. A definite must have to invest in your child's future!

Thank you, Daniel, for ensuring the success of both of my amazing daughters who were accepted into competitive universities on the West and East Coasts!"

— Frances B. in North Carolina

Chapter 9: Knowing When to Retire

"On my first SAT, I scored 1120. With Daniel's help, I was able to improve my superscore to 1330! Daniel helped to demystify the underlying concepts within each question. But even more than that, he let me know when I had peaked, and when it was time to be done with the process."

— S.B. (Class of 2023)

Step 10: Decide If It's Time to Retire

The final piece of the puzzle is knowing when to retire. On the one hand, I don't want to deprive my students of another chance to improve their scores. On the other hand, there comes the point of diminishing returns. Endless effort does not yield endless rewards on a standardized test. And I don't want to over test anyone.

So how can you determine if you should take the test again?

Let's get into it.

How Do Your Real Scores Compare to Your Practice Numbers?

The best barometer you have is to see how your real test scores compare to your practice test scores. Your practice scores give you a sense of where you are on a "good day" vs. a "bad day" vs. a "medium day".

If your real test scores are right in the middle of your practice score range, it might be a judgement call to take the test again. If your real test scores are far below your typical practice scores, then it makes sense to take the test again. And if your real test scores are far better than your typical practice scores, it could be a good indication that you "caught lightning in a bottle".

This is another reason why it's so important to take full length practice tests! They'll help to give you a sense of where your real scores fall within your spectrum of practice numbers.

Let's look at a few examples. I'll start with a case where it was an easy decision to tell my student that she *should* take the test again.

This student's baseline ACT reading score was 22 and her baseline science score was 24. After we worked together, she had scored into the high 20's on several practice tests, along with a few sections in the 30+ range. However, when she sat for the December 2018 ACT, she mismanaged her time on the reading section. This put her into a bad head space, so she was distracted on the science section that followed as well. She scored 24 on the reading and 26 on the science.

We knew that she should take the test again. Why? Because she had many practice scores telling us that she had the potential for more! She just had a bad experience in the testing room. She resumed her practice sections, with a particular focus on timing and pacing. When she took the test again in April of 2019, her reading and science scores both shot up to 34!

This was a clear case of a student who knew she should take the test again. Her December test scores were well below her typical practice numbers. We knew she was capable of further score increases.

(Sidenote – her mother wrote the testimonial at the top of Chapter 8!)

On the other side of the coin, another student kept taking the SAT several times after I told her to retire. She saw significant jumps out of the 1000's into the 1100's, and eventually up to 1250 on the December 2018 test. She had never done that well on her practice tests, so these were her best numbers to date. Plus, *I could see how much she was struggling with the material*. Given both of those points, I advised her to retire with the December numbers. Still, she decided to take the test several more times. She never broke the 1250 mark again.

Granted, I'm not always right! Some students do surprise me.

One of my students was starting with PSAT numbers in the 900's. We worked hard in the fall of his junior year, and he scored 1190 on his October 2018 SAT. Nice jumps already! But he wanted to continue. So we continued our work. On the March 2019 SAT, his 1190 jumped up to 1370! Off the charts.

This could have been a situation where a student might have considered stopping after seeing those initial score jumps. However, he pressed on. This turned out to be the right choice!

So, will some students see continual increases on subsequent attempts? Yes. Will everyone? No. There does come the point of diminishing returns.

The million-dollar question is when might that happen for you? Let's consider what reasonable score increases you can expect, and why the numbers might hit a plateau.

How Much Can Your Score Go Up

I'm not one of those tutors who guarantees a 200-point increase on the SAT or a 6-point increase on the ACT. It happens for some students, but it certainly does not for everyone. Every student is starting in a different place, and every student has a different potential.

Be wary when you see test companies advertise specific score increases.

Granted, I'm not saying that you shouldn't set ambitious goals for yourself. Please do! But also temper that with realistic expectations. To repeat that line from an earlier chapter, "It's a number 2 pencil... not a magic wand."

Instead of hitting an exact number, try to improve half the distance to the 100th percentile. For example, if you're starting in the 50th percentile, you can aim to improve to the 75th percentile. If you're starting in the 80th percentile, you can aim to improve to the 90th percentile.

Just to give this some context of actual numbers: an ACT score jump from 19 to 25 might be comparable to a score jump from 29 to 32. It's not the same as another 6-point jump from 29 to 35. Likewise on the SAT, a 200-point jump from 1000 to 1200 is not comparable to a 200-point jump from 1300 to 1500.

How is that possible? Shouldn't a 6-point jump be the same across the board? Shouldn't a 200-point increase over there be comparable to a 200-point increase over there?

No.

Why?

The curve.

The Curve Gets Nasty at the Top

The SAT and ACT are not designed for perfect scores. It's not like your high school physics class, where everyone might score above a 95 on a given test if you all do well enough. The SAT and ACT distribute their scores according to a standard deviation curve. In a standard deviation distribution, the majority students will score in the middle percentiles, while fewer and fewer score towards each extreme end.

Because of that, a 6-point jump on the ACT from 19 to 25 is far easier than a 6-point jump from 29 to 35. Likewise, it is far easier to improve your score from 1000 to 1200 on the SAT than it is from 1300 to 1500.

Why? Because the top of the scoring curve is very harsh.

Here are some examples from recent tests:

- On a recent SAT, a student who missed only 4 math questions would have lost *90 points!* Ouch. In the middle of the curve, missing 4 questions might only take off 20 or 30 points.
- This is echoed on the ACT as well. On one recent science test, a student who missed only 4 questions would have lost *7 points!* Brutal. In the middle of the curve, missing 4 questions might only take off 2 or 3 points.
- This is also reflected on the digital SAT. On the one of the Bluebook practice tests, a student who misses only 2 verbal questions would lose 50 points right off the bat. The middle of the curve is much kinder.

And this is what happens at the top of the curve. In those top percentiles, you will be penalized much more for just missing a few questions.

This is why a 200-point score jump over here is not comparable to a 200-point score jump over there. In other words, a jump from 1000 to 1200 is not the same as a jump from 1300 to 1500. Likewise on the ACT, where a 6-point jump from 19 to 25 is not an apples-to-apples comparison with a 6-point jump from 29 to 35. It's much more difficult to see those same score increases at the top of the curve.

So rather than having a final score in mind, think about improving your score half the distance to the 100th percentile.

Now, have I seen students do better than that? Yes. Will everyone see those sorts of score increases? No.

Just to use actual numbers, I've had clients starting with SAT scores in the 900's, telling me that they want to break the 1400-mark. Likewise, I've had students with ACT scores in the teens who tell me that they want to break the 30-mark. If they do, I'm honest with them that those are very lofty goals.

So all I'm saying is that it's important to have realistic expectations before you start. Hope for the best, and work hard, but realize that the numbers will plateau at a certain point. This is especially true at the top of the curve, where they will penalize you much more for missing just a small handful of questions.

The ACT and Random Topics

In previous chapters, I mentioned how the ACT is a little "unfair" towards the end of the math sections. It's not just that the last few ACT math questions throw in harder topics. *They throw in random topics*. As such, it's very difficult to anticipate what topics to study to earn those final few points. It's a little luck of the draw in terms of what random topics might appear.

To anticipate some of these math topics, check out this video here! It includes some harder topics that have popped up on recent ACT tests.

https://tinyurl.com/DanFisch15

Timing

Timing struggles can also explain why your scores might hit their ceiling.

Last year, I worked with a student... let's call her Dara. Dara was quite bright, but an extremely slow test taker. On a good day, she was only able to answer about 32 out of 52 reading questions within the time, along with about 30 out of 44 grammar questions. And that was on a good day.

All told, she was able to improve her PSAT score from 1010 to 1200, and her SAT score from 1170 to a superscore of 1340. Huge! This was all the more impressive given the fact that she didn't have time to answer significant portions of the verbal sections. I told her to retire proudly with those score jumps. However, she decided to continue. Her subsequent scores never broke the 1340 mark.

This was a classic case of diminishing returns. It wasn't worth it for Dara to keep sitting for the test when she didn't have time to answer so many questions.

Now, there are some strategies to work around timing struggles. Check out Chapters 11 – 13! Especially the ACT-specific strategies in Chapter 11, where I talk about why to answer the questions out of order.

But even these strategies have their limits. If you don't have time to answer significant portions of each section, the scores will hit a ceiling sooner than later.

What Does Success Look Like for You?

And another point worth noting – your definition of success is specific to you. Your score goals might be very different from those of your friends.

For example, I recently worked with a student who started with a score of 850 on her March '21 exam. She just wanted to break the 1000 mark. We worked hard, and she was able to improve her 850 up to 1020 on the Oct '21 test. She was thrilled! Likewise with another student who improved from 950 to 1120, and another who improved her ACT score from 15 to 21.

Everyone is starting in a different place, with a different goal in mind. That might be breaking the 1000 mark on the SAT or the 20 mark on the ACT. Your score goals are your own.

Think About Where Your Potential Points Are

Another thing to consider is where you still have potential points to gain. Students with lower scores are missing some of the "low-hanging fruit". Which is good news! It means that they have doable points coming from some of the easier topics. However, as they increase their scores, it means that they're racking up on the easier topics. Now they're only missing questions that are conceptual.

For example, let's say that your ACT English score is 19. That means that you have many potential points coming from some of the easier punctuation topics. (Plow through my grammar playlist!) But once you get into the high 20's, and certainly above 30, you're no longer missing the questions that are rule-based. Rather, you're missing the harder questions that are based on editing and organization.

Likewise with the math. If you're scoring on the lower end, it means that there are doable points coming from the easier topics, like isolating a variable, systems of equations, trinomial factoring, etc. (Hit that math playlist!) But once you get into the mid-600's, and certainly into the 700's, the remaining questions are more about problem solving.

Check out that bacteria question again in Chapter 1. It's a good example of the type of question a student might miss at the top of the curve. There's nothing to "study" there; it's more about critical thinking.

Which is not to say that further increases are impossible. Still, those remaining points are more about comprehension than they are about knowledge.

Which leads us to this next point: ability and comprehension.

Ability and Comprehension

At a certain point, it's no longer a matter of memorization or effort. A student might have memorized every math formula in the world and every piece of punctuation. However, at the end of the day, it comes down to innate ability.

And two quick disclaimers for these upcoming examples. I don't tell them to be pessimistic. I tell them:

1. To be fully transparent that yes, there comes a point when a student has scored to the best of his or her ability.
2. To help you with some of these harder concepts! That way, you can avoid making the same mistakes that I'm about to cover.

So think of this section as a mix of love tough and cautionary tales that you can learn from. Here are some common comprehension struggles that I've seen with my students.

Potential Comprehension Struggle 1: Identifying Parts of Speech

I have a great "trick" to help my students remember the difference between *affect* and *effect:* the acronym RAVEN. You can use those letters in the following phrase.

<u>R</u>emember <u>A</u>ffect is a <u>V</u>erb and <u>E</u>ffect is a <u>N</u>oun.

(Sidenote – yes, there are exceptions to that. For example, to *effect* change in society. Or a character in a book might have a certain *affect* about them. However, these exceptions don't come up on the test. For purposes of the ACT, the RAVEN trick will work. Back to my amusing anecdote.)

My students love the RAVEN trick. And for more helpful grammar tricks, check out this video!

https://tinyurl.com/DanFisch16

Why do I bring up this grammar tip here? Well...

In the summer of 2021, I worked with a student... let's call him Matt. Matt had seen some very significant score increases into the 1200+ range. However, his parents had a bit of a "pie-in-the-sky" mindset of "1400 or bust". After his second set of SAT results came out, they called me to chat. They didn't understand how a student with such a high GPA could "only score in the 1200's".

I gave them my usual speech about how a GPA has very little to do with SAT and ACT scores. (Go back to read Chapter 1 for my full thoughts on that point.) Then I reiterated the struggles that Matt was having during our lessons. To illustrate, I brought up a grammar question he had missed on a recent practice test.

I'm paraphrasing for copyright, but the question went something like this: "Person A had an (affect/effect) on Person B".

Now, Matt *totally understood* my RAVEN trick. However, after reading that sample sentence, he interpreted that because Person A was *doing something* to Person B, the sentence must be using that word as a *verb*. So he picked *affect*. He didn't understand that the word was actually being used as a noun in that sentence, so it should have been *effect*.

So even though Matt had memorized the rule, he struggled with the more fundamental skill: identifying parts of speech. This helped the parents understand the nature of their son's struggles.

The father finally asked me, "Are we expecting too much of him?"

My answer was yes.

And is a very common thing I see when my students hit a plateau with their scores. ***It's not a matter of memorization and it's not a matter of effort; it's a matter of ability and comprehension.***

At a certain point, ability and comprehension trump effort and memorization.

Potential Comprehension Struggle 2: Matching Pronouns and Antecedents

Here's another grammar example to illustrate this hurdle. Many of my students struggle with pronouns. When they do, I give them my two standard pronoun examples. Think about what word would go in each of these blanks.

Q. Even though the plantain is tropical, many chefs have worked with _____ before.

Q. Even though plantains are tropical, many chefs have worked with _____ before.

The first sentence is referring to *the plantain*, which is a singular word. So the blank needs a singular pronoun. It should say "... chefs have worked with **_it_** before."

The second sentence is referring to *plantains*, which is plural. So the blank needs a plural pronoun. It should say "... chefs have worked with **_them_** before."

This is called matching a pronoun to an antecedent. (What's that? None of my students from the such-and-such high school have ever seen this before? You don't say. Moving on.) Don't worry about that fancy word "antecedent". Simply put – a singular word over there needs to match with a singular word over there, just as a plural word over there needs to match with a plural word over there.

And many of my students understand these two examples! However, many of them still missed these two questions that came up on recent SAT exams. Once again, I'm paraphrasing for copyright purposes, but the questions went something like this.

Q. When the first 3D printer hit the market, designers complained that the renderings _____ created looked fake.

Q. The fossils that Dr. Grant found led him to conclude that the dinosaurs had lived at the location for centuries, using _____ as a base to graze on the local flora.

I'll give you a minute to think about your answers. I'll be over here checking the sports ball scores.

(Oh good, we traded away our two best pitchers in the same week. Management just said that they don't expect the team to be competitive for another 3 years. Just another day as a Mets fan.)

What is the antecedent in the first sentence? In other words, what's the noun that produced something that looked fake? *The first 3D printer*. So we need a singular pronoun. It should say "... the renderings *it* created looked fake."

But here's the thing: *many of my students didn't understand that the blank was referring to the printer. They thought that the blank was referring to the designers. From there, many students picked the pronoun **they** instead of it.*

And there's nothing to study there. Rather, it's a matter of understanding that *the printer* is creating something that looks fake, and *not the designers*.

Likewise with the next one. Many of my students struggled to understand that the location was the antecedent in that sentence. If *the location* is a singular word, then it should say how "...dinosaurs used *it* as a base."

Now, these same students completely understand my two plantain examples. One plantain = it. Many plantains = them. They totally get that. But on their real tests, they didn't understand what word the pronoun was referring to.

And for more practice with pronouns, watch my video here!

https://tinyurl.com/DanFish17

But the bigger point – it's not a matter of memorizing that *it* is a singular word and *them* is a plural word. It's a matter of ability. Not every student is capable of matching a pronoun to the word that it describes (the antecedent).

Granted, there was that one student who asked me to define what singular and plural meant. But 99.6% of the time, that's not the issue.

Potential Comprehension Struggle 3: Subject-Verb Agreement

I see similar struggles with subject-verb agreement. I won't get into the weeds with examples for this one. Check out my video here! It walks you through my lesson on this topic.

https://tinyurl.com/DanFisch18

A few years ago, I was working with... let's call him Jeff. I liked Jeff. Really. That said, Jeff. Could. Not. Spot. A. Prepositional. Phrase. To. Save. His. Life. And spotting a prepositional phrase is an essential skill for subject-verb agreement.

We looked at three examples in a row. He got it by the third one. Then half an hour later in our lesson, he missed a prepositional phrase that came up on a subsequent question. When I pointed it out, he threw his hands up and shouted in frustration, "...but I'm never going to spot that on the test!!"

And here's the thing: *he wasn't wrong*. That's not meant to be defeatist or critical. Jeff simply could not spot a prepositional phrase on his own.

Now, this is where the cousin questions work their magic! They are designed to help you pattern certain concepts in your brain so you can spot them in the future. Go back to Chapter 7 as needed to review how to incorporate your cousin questions into your practice work.

Still, if I wasn't showing Jeff prepositional phrases on three consecutive cousin questions, he could not spot them.

Again, nothing to "study" here; it comes down to ability. (And do check out that video above for more help on this topic! You'll be spotting prepositional phrases in no time. Unless your name is Jeff. I'm kidding, that wasn't really his name.)

Potential Comprehension Struggle 4: Harder Versions of Possession

Another popular struggle for my students is understanding that inanimate nouns can be possessive. For example, take this sentence:

The tree's leaves are green.

Many of my students struggle to understand that an inanimate object like a tree can be possessive. They only understand possession in the sense of a person owning an object, such as "the boy's book" or "the girl's ball", etc. However, they can't wrap their mind around the tree "owning" the leaves.

So they get questions like this wrong, even though they understand the difference of boys and boy's, or girl's and girls', etc. Super quick tip: inanimate nouns can indeed be possessive! For example, "the tree's leaves" or "the table's edge". The leaves "belong to" the tree, just as the edge "belongs to" the table. Possession can mean more than a person owning an object. (Plus, it's a pretty great Sarah McLachlan song. Another 90's reference, skip it.)

Potential Comprehension Struggle 5: Plain Old Reading Comprehension

And then there is sheer comprehension. On the most semantic level, many of my students simply don't understand what they read. As I said with Jeff a moment ago, that is not meant to be cruel or critical. I'm just the doctor reading the cholesterol report: they don't understand what they read.

In Chapter 1, I told the story of Chloe who had never read a book. As a result, she struggled mightily with the reading passages on the test. Chloe might be an extreme example, but I see this with my students every day.

For example, a recent SAT passage used the phrase "prone to romantic reverie". Many students didn't understand what that meant. (It meant that the character was likely to get lost in her daydreams.)

Now, there are strategies to sidestep struggles with comprehension! Help is coming in Chapter 12. For example, in that chapter, I talk about the importance of *predicting your own answer before looking at the choices*. This helps if you don't know what all of the words mean in the answer choices.

Here's an example of a practice question where my students find this particularly helpful. The question asks what sort of relationship the narrator of the passage has with her father. Many of my students are able to correctly predict that she feels comfortable telling him secrets. From there, the correct answer says that the father is "privy to her confidences". Many of my students don't know what that phrase means. (It means that she's comfortable telling him secrets.) But even if they don't know that, it doesn't matter! *With a solid prediction, they can still knock out the other choices. It's not the three choices over there, so it must be that remaining choice with the weird words over there. That's all that matters!*

So are there ways to sidestep comprehension struggles? Yes. See Chapter 12 for more on this!

That said, it is still imperative to understand what you read, both in the passage and in the questions. At a certain point, comprehension struggles do account for the verbal numbers hitting a plateau.

Potential Comprehension Struggle 6: Math "Choreography"

Math scores can also come down to ability. There are certainly potential points coming from memorizing formulas and learning "tricks". But that's only half the battle. From there, it's about execution.

For example, many of my students have indeed memorized the quadratic formula. However, they still miss questions where they have to use this formula. Why? Because there are so many steps of math "choreography" that follow (how to rationalize a radical, order of operations, how to manipulate a fraction, etc.). Granted, a tutor or teacher can help you with the step-by-step "choreography" of math. Still, many students get stuck in the actual mechanics of working with that formula.

For refresh on those steps, check out the video here!

https://tinyurl.com/DanFisch19

Potential Comprehension Struggle 7: Problem Solving and Logic

Think about the bacteria question we saw in Chapter 1. Again, that question is a perfect example of students getting stumped by problem solving and logic more than memorization or computation. Go back to give it a look; it's a fun one.

Now, don't get lost in the details from these anecdotes. The bigger point is this: there comes a point when your score increases no longer come down to effort, memorization, strategies, or "tricks". They come down to ability and comprehension. To quote Mama Rose, "You either got, or you ain't."

All of that said, I'm not letting you off the hook so easy! Sometimes, *it is indeed all about effort*. Which brings us to a very important question to consider – are you up for it?

Are You Up for It?

The final thing to consider is energy and motivation. Can you give your full effort to another round of testing?

Here are some examples I've seen of my students balking:

- One student told me she simply wouldn't be doing the homework that I assigned.
- Another student told me he flat out refused to do any practice sections.
- Another student told me I couldn't expect him to study the math rules between our lessons.
- Last year, a student told her mother and me that if she took the test again, she would try on the math sections, but not on the verbal sections.

(sigh)

So ask yourself honestly – do you feel like your test scores reflect your best effort? If you don't have the motivation to put in the work, it is indeed time to retire.

On the other side of the coin, disappointing scores are sometimes the exact motivation that my students need! It's not just that these scores scare them into action. (Well, sometimes they do.) Rather, these scores help them understand the effort that they need to start putting in.

Case in point – on the 2019 March SAT, one of my students moved from the 900's on her PSAT to 1100 on the button. Not bad. Still, she was coasting up to that point. Her March scores gave her the incentive (and perhaps fear) she needed to start putting more effort in. On the May 2019 exam, her 1100 jumped to 1310!

Likewise with a previous ACT student. He didn't give much effort to his June 2016 exam, and he scored 19. But the summer going into his senior year, he started to try. On the September 2016 test, his 19 bumped up to 25 (including a 9-point grammar jump).

Granted, I was able to cover much more material with these students between their two exams. But besides that, both of these students decided to "turn on the effort switch" after they got their first set of scores.

There's no motivation like disappointment!

So be honest with yourself – do you have it in you? If you feel motivated, go for it! But if you're spent, that's worth considering as well. And if you're flat out resistant to the process, then yes, you're done.

Plus, think about the other factors from this chapter (timing, where you are in the curve, what sorts of questions you're still missing, etc.).

And above all, think about how your real scores compare to your practice scores. Again, this is why it's so important to take full length practice tests; they'll give you a sense of your scores on a "good day" vs. a "bad day". Stay motivated and work hard, but balance that with reasonable expectations about when the numbers might plateau. Your practice numbers will give you a better sense of that.

> *"I have two daughters, both smart with different studying styles and skillsets. My objective was to maximize their capacity for success on the SAT exam, while ensuring that the process of preparation would not tax them. I did not want their SAT preparation to eclipse their schoolwork, or more importantly, add to their already stressful junior years. In addition, I was well aware that even though their academic experiences were robust, my girls lacked some fundamentals in grammar and math. They certainly had gotten by without having to master some essentials of language and algebra, so I wanted (if possible) for their SAT preparation to fill in these gaps as well.*
>
> *Daniel delivered on all these requirements and more. He developed a clear structure for studying. This process was easily integrated into my girls' regular weeks of schools and extracurriculars. Clearly the SAT homework needed to be completed and a priority, but both commented it was 'fun' and 'enjoyable', especially during such a stressful time in their lives. Time management during the actual test was also emphasized and practiced.*
>
> *Finally, Daniel is a teacher, and his process reflects that. My daughters improved their scores dramatically, but also learned how to better comprehend, analyze, and synthesize – methods in which they continue to excel!"*
>
> — Ann B. (Mother of Students from the Classes of 2012 and 2015)

Chapter 10: Submitting Your Scores

"I thought that we were able to submit just the math scores from one month and just the verbal scores from another month?"

— Many of my Clients

Should I have called this Step # 11? Maybe. But did I prefer having "10 Steps" as a nice round number for the title of my book? Also maybe.

So consider this Step 10-b.

Or a delicious secret menu item.

In any case, let's talk how it works when the time comes to submit your test scores to colleges.

Do You "Have To" Submit All of Your Scores?

My students and their parents often tell me how Aunt Susan told them they "have to" submit all their scores to colleges. Or even more egregious, a guidance counselor told them a college is able to find out test scores they don't submit.

Channeling my inner Dwight Schrute again: false!

When the time comes to submit your scores to colleges, it is up to you to decide which test dates you want to send. If you send the scores from a certain date, a college will see them. If you don't submit the numbers from a certain date, a college will not see them.

Now, there are several caveats that come along with that. We'll get to those in just a moment.

But let's just stay on the point for a moment that you don't "have to" submit all of your scores to colleges. You might have two potential sources of cognitive dissonance here: the practical and the emotional.

Let's untangle both.

On the practical side, I'll make up an extreme example to illustrate. Let's say you take the test nine times. (Please don't, but let's just say you do.) You can choose to submit your scores from *just attempt number seven*. If you do, that's the only set of scores that colleges would see. They would not see your scores from the other eight attempts, nor would they even know that you took the test during those other eight dates.

Students sometimes tell me that a guidance counselor told them something to the effect of, "...but colleges are able to see scores that you don't submit."

No they can't! If you do not submit your scores from a given month, colleges have no way to "press the magic button" to supersede that. They won't even know that you took the test during those other months.

Again, this comes with a few caveats. We'll get there shortly.

And then there's the emotional side. Some students and parents feel like they're "breaking the rules" here. If a college asks to see all of their scores, they feel bad for not submitting them.

I'm not calling these feelings invalid. That said, I genuinely don't consider this to be any major ethical violation. Why?

First – something often goes wrong in the test room! Unfortunately, I have many stories I can tell here. I touched on a few of these back in Chapter 8. Here are just a few favorite examples from my students on their real SAT and ACT exams.

- On one test, a proctor invited a few teachers in the room to have a full-volume conversation while the students were taking the test. My student was quite distracted. As a result, he did not perform as well as he had on previous practice tests.
- On another test, the fire alarm went off. (Everyone was ok.) Still, the students had to leave the room for a bit. When they came back, the proctor did not add that time back to the section! So these students lost a significant chunk of time for that section.
- Another student got a bloody nose in the middle of a test. He left the room to tend to it, so he was only able to answer about half of that section.

And I could go on with other fun test day mishaps.

Also, my students often sit for the test with no intention of sending those scores in the first place! They are sitting for the test as a pressure free "trial run". Obviously, they want to do as well as possible. However, their main goal is to just go through the "choreography" of test day. They are sitting for the test to "get the willies out" so that their next round can be more focused and relaxed.

This is especially true for the TIR reports that we've mentioned in previous chapters. Remember – only certain months offer you the chance to analyze your questions from the ACT. This feature used to be offered in December, April, and June. Starting in 2023, that changed to *September*, April, and June.

So, in September of 2023, several juniors of mine sat for the ACT. *These students were extremely early in their prep process.* So why do it? Because September was the last time until April that they would have the chance to analyze their questions! Their goal was not to be one and done. Rather, they wanted to be able to analyze their TIR reports as a study tool for the next round.

And ditto for my juniors who used to take the October SAT to view their QAS reports, back when that was a thing. See Chapter 7 for my full thoughts on that.

Whatever the circumstances are, I don't think that these students should be forced to submit any scores they don't want to. Especially if something goes wrong in the room, like a talking proctor, a fire drill, or a bloody nose! These students are not being duplicitous and they're not trying to get away with something unethical. They're just waiting to see what all of their scores are so that they can then make a more informed decision.

Or they're just sitting for the test as a pressure free "trial run" to see what the room is like.

Or in the case of the TIR report, they're sitting for the test with the sole intention of getting to analyze their performance so they can better prepare for the next round.

And to paraphrase from Jerry and George – I don't think there's anything wrong with that. (Another callback to the '90s.)

Now, time for the caveats.

Caveat 1: How Superscoring Works

Some colleges allow an option called *superscoring*. Throughout this book, you'll see several testimonials where my students refer to their "superscores".

What's a superscore?

(By the by – my spellcheck hates the word superscore, but that's how the ACT folks spell it on their site. So that's what we're going with. Deal with it, Microsoft Word.)

Superscoring is a policy that allows you to combine your best numbers from different exam dates. Some colleges will consider your final score to be your best verbal score from one test, combined with your best math score from another test.

For example, let's say that in one month, you score 580 on the verbal section and 610 on the math section, for a final score of 1190. Then the next month, let's say that the numbers "see-saw"; the verbal score improves to 620, but the math score dips to 560. This would give you a final score of 1180.

However, the superscore option allows you to mix and match the best scores from each round for a new final score. So using the numbers above, your 610 math score from the first test and your 620 verbal score from the second test would now give you a superscore of 1230.

However, this comes with a critical stipulation: when you submit the scores from a given month, you have to submit all of the scores from that month.

So you can't "cherry pick" your scores. In other words, you can't submit just the verbal numbers from one month, and then just the math numbers from another month. When you submit the scores from a given month, you have to send all of the scores from that month.

This feature on the College Board site is called Score Choice. Be sure to utilize it!

So, colleges that allow the superscore option will consider your final score to be the best numbers from any test you submit. Still, keep in mind they will still be able to see *all* of the scores from any test date you submit.

Simply put – you are either submitting all of the numbers from a given test date, or none of the numbers from a given test date.

Likewise with the ACT. Just to recap, your final ACT composite score is made up of the average of your scores from all four sections. So a 25.25 would round to 25, where a 25.5 would round to 26.

Fractions of a point can indeed make a difference! Superscoring can help you squeak out another point or two on the ACT, depending on how the decimal rounds.

Each college has a different policy on whether or not they'll accept your superscore as your final score. Do your homework for any schools on your list.

Caveat 2: So Don't "Phone It In" on Certain Sections!

Here are some cautionary tales of students who tried to "game" this policy a bit.

In the spring of 2023, I worked with a student who had seen some very significant increases in her math scores. However, she struggled considerably with the timing of her verbal sections. So, she decided to take one more stab at the August 2023 test, with a particular focus on the timing factor in the two verbal sections.

To her credit, she did improve her verbal scores on that test. *But here's the thing: she simply did not try on the two math sections.* She left 11 questions blank (cardinal sin!), and just coasted through sections 3 and 4.

So while her verbal numbers did improve, her 710 math score dipped to 510!!!

This became a bit of a "black eye" on her score report. *If she wanted colleges to see her highest verbal numbers from the August test, she would also have to show them those significantly lower math scores.*

(Let the record show – she did not tell me that she was going to do this! I would have told her not to. I'm giving her a loving slap on the wrist here, as she'd heard my superscore speech many times.)

Likewise with another student on a recent ACT. After taking the February 2021 test, he was happy with his reading score. For the April 2021 exam, he decided to focus primarily on bumping his math and grammar numbers.

And he did!

However, he completely phoned it in for the reading in section 3. His reading score of 28 in February dipped to 15 in April. He simply did not try on that section.

So, don't play with fire with the superscore policy! Or more specifically, *always try on every section.* Yes, if a school utilizes this policy, it will consider your final score to be the best math numbers over here combined with the best verbal numbers over there. *However, the school is still able to see all of the scores from any month you submit!* So don't simply "coast" on one section while trying your hardest on another.

Caveat 3: Forgo the Free Score Submission

When you sign up for the test, you can select the option to send your scores for free to four different colleges. If you select that option, then yes, the scores will be sent without your control. **So never select that option!** Always wait to see what the scores are before deciding which scores to send.

Caveat 4: Submitting Scores Within a School System

Also, if you submit your scores to a college within a certain university system, other schools in that system can then view your scores, too. For example, this might be the case within certain state university systems. Contact each school to see what their policy is on this.

And Some Other Points to Consider

- Your scores from the digital SAT are automatically reported to your high school. Don't worry; they're still not delivered to colleges without your permission.
- In the category of I won't pretend to know something I don't: the College Board practice book mentions that if you forgo the Score Choice option, College Board will then send the scores from your last six tests.

And full disclosure – I'm not quite sure what that means. Do they do this automatically? Or do they mean that if you don't specify which months you want to submit, they'll just send your most recent six tests? I don't know.

Either way, selecting Score Choice will alleviate this problem. So again – always select that option! That way, you can choose which dates you want to submit.

- Starting a few years ago, the ACT started to show your superscore as the default score at the top of your home page. Granted, this is only if you take the test more than once. But if you do, the composite score at the top of your score page will show the superscore that is made up of your best numbers from each test. If you scan down the score page, you can see the scores specific to each test date.
- The ACT had once announced a "section retesting" policy. This was supposed to begin during the September 2020 exam. This policy would have allowed students to come back to take specific sections after they sat for the full exam.

In other words, they would first have to sit for a full ACT exam. Then, at a subsequent exam date, they could have come back to take just the reading and grammar sections, or just the math and science sections, (or any combination of sections they wanted). This way, they wouldn't have to sit for the full test in another attempt to bump their superscore.

However, that didn't materialize. Stay tuned to my social media accounts to see if the ACT folks ever decide to bring back section retesting in the future.

We made it through the ten steps! (And a bonus step 11 at the end there.) Now let's get to some actual lessons.

Part III: Essential Strategies

"Daniel worked with both of my daughters on their SAT and ACT exams. His mastery of this material is impressive, for sure! But more than just knowledge, his real expertise lies in his ability to customize his approach to fit any student's needs. Daniel not only taught my girls what they needed to know for these tests, but also gave them an incredible sense of test-taking confidence, along with other skills to navigate the exams successfully. As a parent, I can't think of anything more valuable when it comes to test prep. I have highly recommended Daniel to several friends over the years because his expertise was truly invaluable. Follow his guidance!"

— Kim G. (Mother of Students in the Class of 2014 and 2016)

In Part I of the book, we talked about how and why the SAT is changing, along with the format of the digital SAT and ACT.

In Part II, we covered a step-by-step timeline of how to make a test prep plan.

In Part III, we'll cover some actual test-taking strategies. Some of these strategies are specific to the digital SAT. Others are specific to the ACT. And plenty of them are relevant for both exams!

Speaking of the digital SAT: while students in the U.S. were still taking the paper test during the spring of 2023, students overseas were the first to see the digital test. Here's a quick success story from an international student of mine who took the digital test during that window.

In the spring of 2023, we worked hard to prepare her for the digital test format. As such, she was able to improve her Bluebook practice scores from 1090 to 1250. Then, on the real digital SAT, her scores improved from 1260 on the June 2023 exam to 1400 on the October 2023 exam.

These upcoming strategies helped her quite a bit! And now, I bring them to you.

In Chapter 11, we'll start with a few rapid-fire hints. In Chapters 12 and 13, we'll do a deep dive into the questions.

Chapter 11: Rapid-Fire Hints

"Daniel is a true expert on test prep. He is extremely thorough and knows exactly what he's talking about. His strategies helped me score a 1550 on the SAT. You should definitely take the opportunity to learn his methods!"

— One of my Students from the Class of 2021

Q. Daniel is writing this chapter in rapid-fire bullet points because:

A) Chapter 12 is loooooooong, so he's trying to balance things out.
B) He's getting hungry for lunch.
C) The quick points speak for themselves.
D) The Met game starts in... (checks watch...) 28 minutes.
E) All of the above.

(The answer is E. But you knew that.)

In all seriousness, here are some great strategies to navigate the digital SAT. Then we'll get to some quick tips for the ACT.

A Recap of the Technical Aspects of the Digital SAT

- The test is section-adaptive. Your performance on the first module dictates what you'll see in the second module.
- You can answer the questions within a module in any order, but you can only work on one module at a time.
- You can highlight questions you'd like to come back to.
- You can strike out answers to eliminate wrong choices.
- Scratch paper will be allowed.
- You'll have a reference table that lists some of the math formulas – use it!
- You can use your own calculator or the one embedded in the testing app.

Hints on Navigating the Digital Sections

- As we've said, don't worry about which "path" you're on. It's nothing you can control in the moment. Do your best on whatever questions you see.
- Don't get caught up on any reading passage that's giving you trouble. Each passage will only have one corresponding question. So if you're completely stuck, put your best guess and move on.

- Likewise, don't stress over any given question; it might be a "pre-test" question that doesn't count towards your score. Remember, there are two of these sprinkled into each module.
- That said, you won't know which ones they are, so try your best on every question.
- And don't cheat off the person sitting next to you! That student is not necessarily taking the same test as you.

(Plus, you know, the whole morality thing.)

If You're Pressed for Time

- If you're short on time in a verbal module, try to hit any remaining punctuation questions. You can handle those questions more quickly than the longer rhetorical synthesis questions. (More on those questions in the next chapter!)
- If you're pressed for time in a math module, jump around to any topics that look familiar.
- Don't leave any questions blank! Ditto for the ACT. There is no wrong answer penalty. Always put *something* down.
- And if you do need to guess on a math question, put a *good* guess.

For example, consider $x°$ in this picture. Let's say you had no idea how to do the question, or you only had 37 seconds left. What's a decent guess?

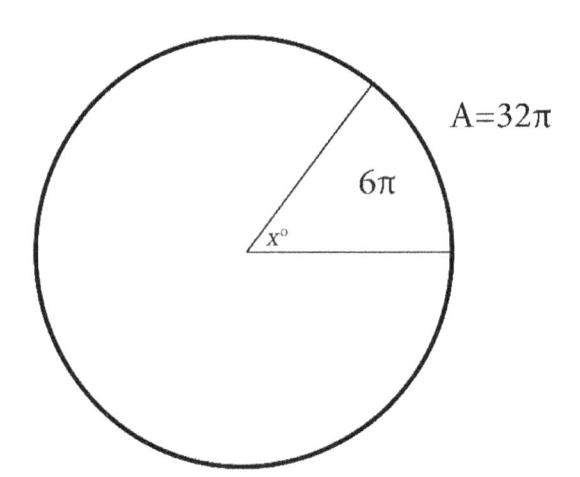

Just by giving it a quick look, you can infer that it is an acute angle. You might guess something like 40° or 50°. Those are decent guesses, based on visualization alone. You're not going to guess something like 163 for that question, nor would you guess 2.5. Those are way off.

Indeed, you can often *eyeball* many diagrams! Granted, they are not always drawn to scale. Even so, you can often estimate a number at least "in the ballpark" of the correct answer.

And speaking of being in the ballpark, pretend a tough trig question was asking for the sine, cosine, or tangent of an angle. What sort of guess would you put?

Sine, cosine, and tangent are *fractions*. So maybe you'd guess ½. Maybe you'd guess ¼. Those are decent guesses! You're not going to guess 37 for a question like that.

Avoiding Careless Errors on the Math

- Answer *exactly* what they're asking for. So if they ask for something like "What is the value of $x + 5$?", I guarantee that a wrong answer choice will just list the value of x. Likewise, if they ask for a shaded area, an answer trap will list the nonshaded area. Reread the question as needed to make sure you've solved for *exactly* what they want.
- Remember, the math questions get harder as you move through each module. Use that as a clue to consider whether you're in an "easy stretch" vs. a "tough stretch". For example, pretend you saw this question at the end of a math module.

$$\sqrt{x^{16}} =$$

It's tempting to say x^4, but the answer is x^8! (Think about what multiplied by itself would give us x^{16}? *When you multiply common bases, you don't multiply the powers; you add them!* So x^8 times itself would be x^{16}.)

Now, don't worry about that math. The point is this: you can trust your instinct at the top of a math section. However, look out for some "trickery" towards the end of the section. They're not supposed to be so easy.

- Your calculator does not always recognize the order of operations. For example:

In the function $f(x) = x^2 + 3x + c$, what is the value of c if $f(-4) = 9$?

The first step is to plug in -4 for x. Your calculator might not recognize what you mean by -4^2. More specifically, it might think that you want to negate 16, giving you -16 instead of 16. Be very careful with the order of operations on your calculator.

- Make sure your calculator is in *degrees* and not *radians*. This is especially important if you usually have your calculator set to radians for your high school math class or physics class.

Rules for the Grid-In Questions

- Some of the math questions will be multiple choice, but others will be "grid-in" questions, where you actually have to bubble in a numeric answer.
- You can bubble in up to five characters (the old test used to only allow four).
- You can get negative answers here (another change from the old test).
- Some questions will ask, "What is one possible value of blah blah blah?" That means there is more than one possible answer. You only have to put one.
- The computer does not know how to read mixed fractions! For example, if you get an answer of 4 and ½, you cannot grid 41/2, because the computer thinks that you mean 41 over 2. You have to convert it to a decimal (4.5) or an improper fraction (9/2).

Essential Strategies for the ACT

(I'm going back to prose now.)

The rest of this chapter contains strategies that are specific to the ACT. If you know you're only doing the SAT, you can skip to the next chapter. If the ACT is also on your to-do list, read on!

On the ACT English section (section 1), *do not answer the grammar questions in order*. Instead, answer the "quick-fix" questions in tandem with the passage. In other words, read a bit of the passage... and answer the quick-fix questions that correspond to that portion. Then read a bit more of the passage... answer the quick fix-questions that correspond to that portion, etc. Continue this way throughout the passage.

However, *skip any questions that deal with organization, comprehension, transitions, or shuffling sentences around.*

For example, skip any questions that ask something like "where should sentence 5 most logically be placed" or "which of the following best establishes the main idea of the following paragraph".

Why? Because you don't have enough information to answer those questions yet! You need to read the full passage to understand the organization questions.

So answer the quick-fixes in tandem with the passage... skip the organization questions... finish the passage... and before moving on to the next passage, do a second pass at the organization questions. This way, you have more context to understand them!

(And it's also more time efficient.)

Likewise, don't do the reading questions in order either. Somewhere in the ACT reading section (section 3), you'll find the paired passage. This is where they give you two smaller passages to compare, written by two different authors.

You shouldn't read the two paired passages consecutively. Instead, after you read the first passage, skip the second passage! Move right along to answer the questions that just ask about passage 1. Why? So that it's fresh in your brain! No need to confuse yourself with passage 2. Who cares about passage 2! You don't need to know it to answer the questions from passage 1.

So read passage 1... answer the passage 1 questions... *then* read passage 2... answer the passage 2 questions... and then answer the questions that deal with both. This way, each passage is fresh in your mind, and you're less likely to confuse the two passages.

And here's another tip for the paired passage: *do it last*. The paired passage can appear as any of the four passages on the ACT. As we've said, timing is often the critical factor on the ACT. Doing the paired passage last helps you have time for at least *half* of the paired passage, rather than *none* of the paired passage.

In other words, let's say that the paired passage was the third of the four passages. You would work through passages one, two, and four normally. Then you'd move to the paired passage. This way, if you're in a time crunch, you can at least read the first of the paired passages and knock out those questions! *This is far better than having to rush on an entire full passage. By doing the paired passage last, you can potentially answer four or five more questions before time is up.*

And if you're running short on time on any ACT sections, jump around to any "quick points". For example, some of the science questions just want you to read a chart or a graph. Jump to those! Likewise, bounce around to any math questions where the topics look more familiar. Stay aware of the clock, and with less than 5 minutes left, try to hit any remaining quick points.

And with less than 2 minutes left, fill in answers for all remaining questions. There is no answer penalty on the ACT, so *never* leave a question blank.

(Two hours later, and the Mets are about to get swept by the Tigers. Why do I even bother?)

(All due respect to those of you from Detroit.)

Chapter 12: Your Verbal Section Toolbox

"There are two types of people: those who can make inferences from the given data."

In this chapter, I'll cover every type of verbal question that appears on the digital SAT, along with the best strategies to use for each.

(And I'm keeping this intro short because we have a lot to do here.)

Quick Domain Recap

In Chapter 3, we mentioned how the verbal questions are arranged throughout each module. Reread that section as needed.

In that chapter, we discussed how the verbal questions are categorized into four different domains.

Domain 1:   Craft and Structure
Domain 2:   Information and Ideas
Domain 3:   Standard English Conventions
Domain 4:   Expression of Ideas

The first two domains make up your reading score. The second two make up your writing score.

Within those domains, College Board uses different titles to categorize each type of question. However, I'm not going to use their titles here. Why? Because they often use the same title to describe different types of questions! For example, they use the title "Words in Context" to describe different types of questions.

So instead, I'm going to use my own titles for each type of question. Plus, some great strategies on how to handle each.

Some Ground Rules for this Chapter

Ground Rule 1: Don't read this chapter passively. Rather, engage with each question. Do your best to answer each before reading ahead to the answer.

Ground Rule 2: I'm not going to organize the questions by domain. Instead, I'll group them together by common strategies and approaches.

Ground Rule 3: This chapter is meant to familiarize you with every type of verbal question you'll see. Check out my grammar playlist for a deeper dive into my grammar lessons! This video will bring you there. (And it's a very popular rule!)

https://tinyurl.com/DanFisch20

Ok, here we go.

Strategy 1: Predicting to Fill in a Word

For many verbal questions, it will help you to predict your own answer before looking at the answer choices. In fact, use your hand to cover the answers! This will mean to cover a part of the screen during the digital SAT. Don't worry about looking silly – do it!

Covering the answers to predict your own answer is critical for several reasons:

1. If you come up with your own answer first, it will be easier to spot the choice that matches your prediction.
2. There are wrong answer traps that they want you to see. By having a prediction, you're less likely to fall for one of these wrong answers.
3. (I'll tell you in a few pages.)

Here are the questions where predicting an answer will help you.

Question Type: Vocab-in-Context

The Vocab-in-Context questions will ask you to define how a word is being used in a given context. These are a carryover from the paper test, and they still appear on the ACT as well. Here's an example.

And use your hand to cover the answers as you read the question!

Q. The first rings that Sauron made were mere **essays** in the craft. It was not until he made the master ring that he was able to wield dominion over all things.

As used in the text, what does the word "essays" most nearly mean?

- A. papers
- B. writing samples
- C. attempts
- D. compositions

Always predict your own answer before looking at the choices. Why? Because if you don't, they're going to tempt you with the most literal definition in the choices.

Case in point, look at choices A, B, and D. These are all variations of the literal definition of an essay. However, that's not how they're using the word in this sentence. Instead, you might predict something like "Sauron was giving it a shot" or "taking a stab at it". The answer is C. Sauron is making an attempt at something; he's not writing a paper for his English class. The word "essay" can have an alternate meaning of an attempt or a try.

And I don't like to use the word *never*. But for the Vocab-in-Context questions, I'll say that the literal definition is *rarely* the answer. So, always cover the answers and predict! This helps you avoid the answer traps they want you to see.

For more practice with the Vocab-in-Context questions, check out this video here. It also covers some other common reading traps.

https://tinyurl.com/DanFisch21

Question Type: Sentence Completions

These are essentially fill in the blank questions. They used to appear on previous versions of the SAT, but they disappeared in 2016 when the 2400-scale test was replaced by the 1600-scale test. So for those of us in the test prep industry, it's nice to see our old friend again.

They will look like this. Once again, use your hand and cover up those answers!

Q. Diana brought a sense of energy to the otherwise _____ classroom.

Which choice completes the text with the most logical and precise word or phrase?

- A. beneficial
- B. staid
- C. cranky
- D. intelligent

Using the clues in the sentence, you might predict something like "dull" or "lifeless". From there, you might not know what that weird word means in choice B. But who cares! You can eliminate the other choices. They don't make sense here. That means the answer is B. And who cares what that weird word means.

So, going back to the third reason that I hinted at a few pages ago: this is why it's so helpful to predict! **You don't necessarily have to know what the answer means. You just have to know that it's not the other choices.** Predicting your own answer will help you with this.

Question Type: Transitions

These questions will ask you to pick the most logical transition between thoughts. Here's an example. And I know I don't need to tell you – cover those answers.

Q. David Pumpkins defies description: he utters a strange catchphrase, wears a bizarre suit, and dances with eerie beatbox skeletons. _____, he can be called his own thing.

Which choice completes the text with the most logical transition?

- A. Regardless
- B. In short
- C. Alternately
- D. Meanwhile

Once again, predicting will help you. More specifically, ask yourself, what is the relationship between the thoughts? The second sentence is summarizing the examples that are given in the previous sentence. So you want to predict a word that conveys that idea. The answer is B.

For more practice with the transitions, check out this video.

https://tinyurl.com/DanFisch22

Plus, that video has a fun little exercise for how the transitions can help you "be psychic" while working on the reading questions. I'm kidding… but I'm not!

Strategy 2: Predicting to Fill in an Idea

On harder questions, you'll not only want to predict a word, but you'll want to predict a full idea. This gets a bit more challenging, but it's just an extension of the previous strategy. Here are some questions that fall into this category.

Question Type: Which Quotation Illustrates the Claim

These questions will ask you to think about how an author might finish his or her own point. Here's an example.

Q. In November of 2021, theater historian Jill Rafson conducted an interview with composer Stephen Sondheim. During their discussion, Sondheim described how writing is a delicate balance between a genuine desire to spread joy and a vainer impulse to be self-indulgent: _____

Which quotation from that interview effectively illustrates the claim?

- A. "There's that first moment, the first flush, the falling in love. But you have to let it cook and see if you still love it in the morning."
- B. "I hate writing; I love having written."
- C. "The hard part is the execution. But even that is fun. When I say fun, of course, I'm talking about agonizing fun. It's not pleasant fun."
- D. "Because it's a form of showing off, but it's also a form of sharing. You want to say, 'Hey, I caught this moment!' It's a wonderful feeling."

Try to predict! The key is right before the blank, "…a balance between a genuine desire to spread joy and a vainer impulse to be self-indulgent". So you want a choice that conveys that idea. The answer is D. That quote explains how writing is both a selfish and a generous act.

Question Type: Complete the Text

These questions are another variation of finishing the author's point. Let's give it a shot.

Again, see if you can think of an idea that could go in the blank *before* you read the answers.

Q. Many who listen to Rod Engeman's financial podcast enjoy his weekly interview with his wife Jean. In those interviews, Jean shares her knowledge about yoga, mindfulness, and macrobiotic cooking. Given the content of those interviews, many might not realize that Jean is also an accomplished financial planner herself! After all, Jean and Rod were both cofounders of their financial planning firm. As such, the listeners who only hear Jean's brief interviews on Rod's podcast might _____

Which choice most logically completes the text?

  A. misinterpret the reasons why Rod founded his firm.
  B. not fully appreciate Jean's contributions to the financial planning field.
  C. assume that Jean's knowledge of the field is superior to that of Rod.
  D. overestimate Jean's financial acumen.

Predict, predict, predict! Those words "as such" are a very important clue. They indicate that the final sentence is going to be an extension of the previous two sentences. The previous two sentences explain that the podcast listeners might only be familiar with Jean's work outside of the financial planning arena. So what can you predict? "As such, the listeners might…"

You might predict something like "the listeners might not realize that she's also an accomplished financial planner". The answer is B. Choices A and C miss the point, and D is the opposite of what the author is trying to say.

Question Type: What Finding Would Support (or Weaken) the Author's Claim

This type of question is an extension of the previous two. It wants you to think about what sort of evidence would help prove or disprove the author's point. They might ask something like:

- Which finding, if true, would most strongly support the scientist's claim?
- Which finding, if true, would most directly undermine the researcher's hypothesis?

Here's an example. Cover those answers!

Q. Many scientists will tell you that our moon was formed by a collision between the Earth and a rogue planet named Theia. This is called The Impact Hypothesis. According to this theory, Theia struck the Earth at an oblique angle about 4.5 billion years ago, sending a large amount of debris into space. This debris eventually coalesced and became our moon. However, in recent years, The Capture Hypothesis has emerged as a more likely explanation for the moon's creation. This theory states that the moon originated elsewhere in our galaxy. Then, while traveling past the earth, the moon got trapped in our planet's gravity about 4.5 billion years ago.

Which finding, if true, would most directly weaken the author's claim?

A. If an object as large as Theia had struck the Earth at an oblique angle, both planets would likely have been destroyed.
B. 4.5 billion years ago, the Earth was too small to have sufficiency gravity to capture an object the size of the moon.
C. The chemical composition of the Earth is much different than that of the moon.
D. There is no impact crater to indicate where Theia might have struck the Earth.

This author is in favor of The Capture Hypothesis. The question wants you to pick a choice that would *weaken* this argument. So you either want to show that:

- The Capture Hypothesis *is not* true...
- ...or that The Impact Hypothesis *is* true.

The answer is B. If the Earth was too small to have sufficient gravity to capture the moon, that would very much weaken The Capture Hypothesis. Choices A, C, and D all provide evidence against The Impact Hypothesis, which would help the author's point.

Strategy 3: Read the Question First!

For many reading questions, it will help you to read the question *before* reading the passage. Why? Reading the question tells you what to look for while reading the passage!

This is particularly helpful on the next four types of questions.

Question Type: Main Idea

These questions are asking for just that – the main idea of the passage. This is why it's so helpful to read the question *before* you read the text! By doing this, you won't get caught up on the details. Instead, you can just read the passage for the central idea.

Give it a shot on this one. (And jump down to read the question *before* you read the passage!)

Q. The following text is adapted from Walt Whitman's poem "Song of Myself". The poem is a sprawling meditation on life. This is the fifty-second and final section.

> I depart as air, I shake my white locks at the runaway sun,
> I effuse my flesh in eddies, and drift in lacy jags.
> I bequeath myself to the dirt and grow from the grass I love,
> If you want me again look for me under your boot-soles.
> You will hardly know who I am or what I mean,
> But I shall be good health to you, nevertheless.
> Failing to fetch me at first keep encouraged,
> Missing me one place search another,
> I stop somewhere waiting for you.

Which choice best states the main idea of the text?

   A. Whitman expresses his love and appreciation of nature.
   B. Whitman laments his own demise, eventually spiraling into despair.
   C. Whitman notes that even though he may perish, a part of his spirit will endure.
   D. Whitman grows increasingly frustrated by the impermanence of all things.

There might be some fairly heady symbolism here. Still the main idea of the text is that Whitman is trying to stay hopeful in the face of death. Even though he will die, he remains optimistic that the reader will still be able to find him. The answer is C.

Question Type: Main Structure or Overall Structure

These questions will ask you to identify the overall structure of the passage. Again, it helps to know that before you read the passage! Give it a shot. (And once again, skip ahead to read the question itself *before* reading the text.)

Q. The following text is adapted from Myra Viola Wilds' poem "Thoughts".

> What kind of thoughts now, do you carry
> In your travels day by day
> Are they bright and lofty visions,
> Or neglected, gone astray?
>
> Matters not how great in fancy
> Or what deeds of skill you've wrought;
> Man, though high may be his station,
> Is no better than his thoughts.
>
> Catch your thoughts and hold them tightly,
> Let each one an honor be;
> Purge them, scourge them, burnish brightly,
> Then in love set each one free.

Which choice best describes the overall structure of the text?

A. It establishes a sense of hope, and then portrays a feeling of regret.
B. It asks that we consider our thoughts, then suggests that we have the grace to not be consumed by them.
C. It personifies our thoughts as living objects, then explains the danger of doing so.
D. It discusses how our thoughts influence our actions, then describes the downside of the human condition.

Once again, you'll have to wade through some symbolism here. Still, the passage is explaining how we must find the balance between valuing our thoughts and not letting them rule our lives. The answer is B.

But even if you missed that, that's ok. As long as you take the point – it's helpful to read the question *before* reading the passage!

This strategy is particularly important on the next type of question.

Question Type: Cross-Text Connections

The Cross-Text-Connections questions will present two short passages, each written by a different author. The question will then ask you to interpret how the author of one text would feel about something from the other text. Here's an example.

(And I know you know – read the question first!)

Q. **Text 1**

The years of James Monroe's presidency are referred to as "The Era of Good Feeling". Having just won The War of 1812, Americans felt a new sense of nationalism; for the first time, people considered themselves Americans before statesmen. Also, Monroe himself was very popular. He won over 80% of the popular vote in the 1816 election, and 228 of 231 electoral votes in the 1820 election. He even embarked on a good will tour, making speeches across the country and impressing people with his demeanor.

Text 2

"The Era of Good Feeling", associated with the presidency of James Monroe, could be considered a bit of a misnomer. This title was coined by a newspaper a mere 5 months after Monroe took office. Shortly after, worries about the national bank's solvency would set off a major economic depression. As a result, cotton prices dropped almost 50 percent, unemployment grew, and many states fell into bankruptcy. Granted, there was improved infrastructure during this time. The success of the Erie Canal opened a surge of western expansion and made New York the busiest port in America. This did give New Yorkers a sense of pride, but it also increased their feelings of sectionalism.

Based on the texts, what would the author of Text 2 most likely say about Text 1's characterization of American nationalism?

- A. It is understandable, given that Americans experienced a shared sense of purpose after The War of 1812.
- B. It is a perspective that the author himself wishes he could adopt.
- C. It is overly optimistic, given that parts of the country still valued their sense of state pride over national pride.
- D. It is unexpected, given the financial struggles that the country was facing.

Notice how helpful it is to read the question *before* reading the passage. "What would the second author say about this idea by the first author?" This gives you a great head start because it tells you what to look for in the middle of all these details!

In these texts, the authors do agree that there were positive aspects of American nationalism. However, author 1 is just summarizing these points. Author 2 is much more critical of them. The answer is C.

And careful of choice D! The second author does indeed mention that the country was experiencing financial struggles. However, he wouldn't cite that as the reason why Americans placed an emphasis on state pride over national pride. This is a popular type of answer trap: they give you true information from the passage, but it doesn't answer the question. Tricky!

Question Type: Rhetorical Synthesis

For the Rhetorical Synthesis questions, you'll *really* want to read the question first. Why? Because they're going to throw a lot of useless information at you.

These questions will list notes that a hypothetical student took while researching a topic. Then, they will ask you to use that information to make a certain point.

Here's an example. (And one more time, skip right to the question!)

Q. While researching a topic, a student has taken the following notes.

- The Verrazzano-Narrows Bridge is a suspension bridge in New York.
- It connects the boroughs of Brooklyn and Staten Island.
- It is 4,258 feet long.
- The Golden Gate Bridge is a suspension bridge in California.
- It connects the city of San Francisco to Marin County.
- It is 4,199 feet long.

The student wants to compare the lengths of the two suspension bridges. Which choice most effectively uses relevant information from the notes to accomplish this goal?

   A. Many suspension bridges, including one that connects San Francisco to Marin County, are longer than 4,000 feet.
   B. The Verrazzano-Narrows Bridge is 4,258 feet long, while the slightly shorter Golden Gate Bridge is 4,199 feet long.
   C. The Verrazano-Narrows Bridge, which is 4,258 feet long, connects the boroughs of Brooklyn and Staten Island.
   D. Both New York's Verrazzano-Narrows Bridge and California's Golden Gate Bridge are examples of suspension bridges.

All of the answer choices might list correct information. There's nothing "wrong" with them factually. However, they specifically want you to compare the lengths of the two suspension bridges. The answer is B.

Jumping right to the question helps you focus on the relevant details and discard the rest.

Strategy 4: Reading with a VERB in Mind

Another great strategy is to read the passages with a *verb* in mind. In other words – don't just try to summarize the passage. Instead, try to think about what the author is *doing*. From there, see if you can explain what the author is doing *with a verb*. For example:

- The author is *defending* her idea that (blah blah blah).
- The author is *refuting* the theory of blah blah blah).
- The author is *elaborating* the reasons for (blah blah blah).

Why are verbs great? Well, here is a preview of the language that they'll use in the upcoming questions:

- What is the main purpose of the text?
- What is the function of the underlined text?
- Why would character A react this way to character B?

Notice the language here. They are not asking you to simply summarize the details. *They are asking you to explain the purpose behind those details.* What is the purpose of this? What is the function of that? Why would this character do this?

Summarizing with a verb automatically puts you into that mindset! Verbs will help you explain purpose and function.

Give it a shot on these next three types of questions.

"Both of my daughters had the privilege of working with Daniel to prepare for the SAT exam. Daniel has a unique ability to tune into a student's thought process, and then shows them helpful strategies to arrive at the correct response while utilizing their time efficiently. In addition, Daniel has an incredible number of tips and strategies on how to take the test itself. My daughters still refer to Daniel's grammar rules for their writing assignments in college! We are so excited that Daniel is sharing his expertise here. Having all of his knowledge in one place will absolutely prepare your student for success."

— D.G. (Mother of Students from the Classes of 2019 and 2022)

Question Type: Main Purpose

These questions will ask just that – what is the main purpose of the text? Give it a shot. (Yes, this is another James Monroe example. For those keeping score, both Monroe questions are taken from my A.P. history papers.)

Q. The following text is adapted from James Monroe's Speech to The House of Representatives on May 4, 1822.

> Having considered the bill entitled, "An Act for the Preservation and Repair of the Cumberland Road", it is with deep regret that I am compelled to object to its passage, under the conviction that Congress does not possess the power under the Constitution to pass such a law. A power to establish turnpikes with gates and tolls and to enforce the collection of tolls and penalties implies a power to adopt and execute a complete system of internal improvement.... I am of the opinion that Congress does not possess this power, and that states individually cannot grant it. The power can only be granted by an amendment to the Constitution.

Which choice best states the main purpose of the text?

- A. To criticize the creators of the Constitution for leaving such a loophole.
- B. To question the authority of individual states.
- C. To call attention to the country's need for better infrastructure.
- D. To explain a rationale as to why Congress does not have the authority to pass such a law.

So many details! Turnpikes this...Constitution that... blah blah blah. Don't get caught up on those details! It is far more important to ask *why* Monroe is writing this. Let's try some verbs:

- To *defend* his decision.
- To *explain* why he is against passing this bill.
- To *clarify* his thought process.

These verbs help you get right to the core of his argument! The answer is D.

Stay in the verb-mindset on the next one as well.

Question Type: The Function of the Underlined Portion

These questions will ask how a certain phrase is functioning within a passage. And notice that language – "function". What is its function? *Its function is to do something.* So verbs will help you here as well!

Have at it.

Q. The following is a transcription of Ben Rice's podcast from April 2, 2023. Ben produces a daily podcast, where he addresses topics such as innovation and exponential technologies.

Are you worried about job security? You should be. Exponential technologies are replacing the need for human labor every day. Folks used to worry that this would only affect jobs in the manual labor sector, such as packaging or production line assembly. But the future is now! Exponential technologies are now engaging in more cerebral jobs. In fact – the entire script of today's podcast was written by Chat GPT, an artificial intelligence program capable of writing tasks that were once thought impossible for a computer to perform. <u>Ben himself took the day off</u>. He told Chat GPT what points he wanted to cover in today's podcast. Chat GPT was then able to search the web and compose a full podcast script in a manner of seconds. Ben then used an audio program to clone his voice and read that script.

Ben will be back tomorrow.

Or will he?

Which choice best states the function of the underlined sentence in the text as a whole?

- A. It emphasizes the surprise that was revealed in the previous sentence.
- B. It introduces a concept that the next sentence then elaborates.
- C. It implies that Ben is irresponsible when it comes to time management.
- D. It sheds light on a challenge facing the modern workforce.

What's the point of telling us that Ben took the day off? Let's think of some fun verbs.

- It *excites* us with a spicy detail.
- It *surprises* us with an intriguing reveal.
- It *heightens* the sense of importance of this new technology.

The podcast script wasn't written by a human; it was written by a computer program. The fact that Ben took the day off amplifies the novelty of that idea. The answer is A.

Choice C misses the point. And choice D is a bit tricky – the full passage does shed light on that challenge, but the underlined portion does not.

And staying in verb-land, one more.

Question Type: Why Would...

These questions can take several forms. For example, these questions might use language like this:

- According to the text, what is true about Stella?
- How would the ambassador respond to the newscast?
- Why would a submarine built with these specifications find it difficult to navigate this new environment?

Notice the language here. "How would this character feel?" or "why would this be true?" Summarizing with a verb really helps with questions that are dealing with *how* and *why* questions! Let's see how.

Q. In Sunken Meadow Park, you will find the beautiful but decrepit Rubicka – a gathering of approximately 1,200 trees. What makes these trees so remarkable is that they are actually one single organism! Every tree in the Rubicka colony grows out of the same cluster of roots. Unfortunately, the Ronkonkoma weasel has been eating away at this root system for the last decade. Twenty years ago, the weasel population was kept in check by larger predators, such as the lynx and the honey badger. In more recent years, however, these predators have dwindled. This has caused a surge in the weasel population.

According to the text, why is Rubicka dying out?

   A. Because the Ronkonkoma weasel has significantly changed its diet
   B. Because these trees have trouble getting sufficient sunlight
   C. Because the root system has lost its main source of nourishment
   D. Because the loss of certain animals has led to other repercussions in other parts of the food chain

There is that *why* language again. A verb will help you answer this more directly!

I'll give you a minute on this one. Take a moment and give it a shot.

(I'm thanking myself for holding on to all of my A.P. papers from high school.)

You might predict something like the author is *explaining* how the loss of certain predators has affected the weasel population, which in turn has led to the decline of Rubicka. The answer is D.

So, verbs are your friend! **The more you can use verbs in your summaries, the more you'll be able to understand the purpose of the details, rather than the details themselves.**

This is especially helpful for the questions that deal with function and purpose!

Strategy 5: On the Grammar Questions – Let the Choices "Announce" The Rule

A quick anecdote – a few years ago, I was working with a student... let's call him Quinn. While working with Quinn, I noticed something interesting. When we reviewed the grammar rules, he was pretty good at recapping them. Still, he would miss many punctuation questions on his practice tests.

For example, I would ask him about the rules for commas and semicolons. He would tell me, correctly, "You can use a comma between a full thought and a not full thought. You can use a semicolon between two full thoughts."

And he was right! But he would still miss these questions fairly often. I asked why he thought that was. He responded, "When I'm taking the test, I'm not like... looking for rules."

And then I had a heart attack.

When I came back to life, I asked him, "Quinn – it goes against my training to ask a yes/no question, but I'm going to. So when you see that one answer choice has a comma and the other has a semicolon, do you recognize that you need to determine whether or not you have full thoughts?"

He said no.

Aha!!!

And that's when I realized that I was taking this skill of *rule recognition* for granted with him. Yes, he was indeed able to tell me many of the rules of punctuation that we'd covered. Still, he didn't realize that he was *supposed to be identifying them within the questions.*

So, *let the answer choices "announce" what rule is in play!*

For example, if you see comma vs. semicolon, you should be asking if you have full thoughts vs. not full thoughts!

If you see "it" vs. "they", you should ask if you need a singular word vs. a plural word.

If you see "boy's" vs. "boys", you should ask if you need a possessive word or a plural word.

Every question based on a grammar rule should prompt the response, "They're showing me A, so I better think about B."

Now, for some of you, I just gave you the most obvious advice in the world. But over the years, I've realized that Quinn was not alone in this struggle! I've seen many other students have the same roadblock. They did indeed know a rule, *but they didn't realize they were supposed to be looking for those rules within the question.*

That's exactly what you're supposed to be doing.

Let's give it a try.

Question Type: Grammar Ala Punctuation

Just to recap from a moment ago, commas can be used between a full thought and a not full thought (in either order). Semicolons can only be used between two full thoughts. Give it a shot.

Q. Trees can have a great variety of life spans. The black willow *(salix nigra)*, for instance, can survive for about 75 _____ giant sequoias *(sequoiadendron giganteum)* can survive for over 3,000 years.

Which choice completes the text so that it conforms to the conventions of Standard English?

- A. years: while
- B. years; while
- C. years. While
- D. years, while

Notice the punctuation that is listed here: a colon, a semicolon, a period, and a comma. This is a very strong clue that you need to identify whether or not you have full thoughts!

So let's read each part separately. "The black willow *(salix nigra)*, for instance, can survive for about 75 years". That **is** a full thought. Now the second part. "While giant sequoias *(sequoiadendron giganteum)* can survive for over 3,000 years". That **is not** a full thought. Therefore the answer is D. A comma fits nicely between a full thought and a not full thought.

And for a deeper dive into this punctuation lesson, check out my video here!

https://tinyurl.com/DanFisch23

So, when you see comma vs. semicolon, you need to check whether or not you have full thoughts. This concept of *spotting the rule* will help you on the next question as well.

Question Type: Grammar Ala Form, Sense, and Structure

I won't give the rule away for this one. I'll just give you the hint that we saw it in an earlier chapter.

Q. Even though it is abundant throughout Alaska, _____ causing disorientation, starvation, and eventually death.

Which choice completes the text so that it conforms to the conventions of Standard English?

- A. the sweet pea plant *(hedysarum alpinum)* is not a viable food source for hikers,
- B. the lateral veins of the sweet pea plant *(hedysarum alpinum)* indicate that it is inedible for hikers,
- C. hikers should not eat the sweet pea plant *(hedysarum alpinum)*,
- D. it is unsafe for hikers to consume the sweet pea plant *(hedysarum alpinum)*,

What clues do you see? Each choice introduces a new subject. Therefore, you have to think about what word the introductory phrase is describing.

This is a cousin of Australia's Bird from Chapter 7! Remember – an introductory phrase must be followed by the noun it describes. For more help with this concept, check out my video here.

https://tinyurl.com/DanFisch24

The sentence starts: "Even though it is abundant throughout Alaska...". What noun is abundant throughout Alaska? The sweet pea plant! That's the noun that has to follow the intro. The answer is A. Choice B makes it sound like the lateral veins are abundant throughout Alaska. Choice C makes it sound like hikers are abundant throughout Alaska.

So, back to the bigger point: **for every grammar question, ask yourself what bell it is ringing.**

As Quinn said, "I'm not like... looking for rules." *But that's exactly what you have to be doing!* Let the clues in the answer choices "announce" what rule is in play.

Strategy 6: Look for Trends or Patterns in the Data

Other verbal questions will ask you to interpret information from charts, graphs, or tables. The key is to ask yourself what trend or pattern you can infer.

Here's an example.

Q. A biology student wanted to see how the presence of frogs in an ecosystem would affect the grasshopper population. To test this, the student sectioned off two areas of his backyard. He placed 100 grasshoppers into both sections, but he only placed frogs into one section. He then tracked the grasshopper population in each section over the course of 15 days. At the end of the experiment, the student posited that the frogs were the only reason why the grasshopper populations decreased.

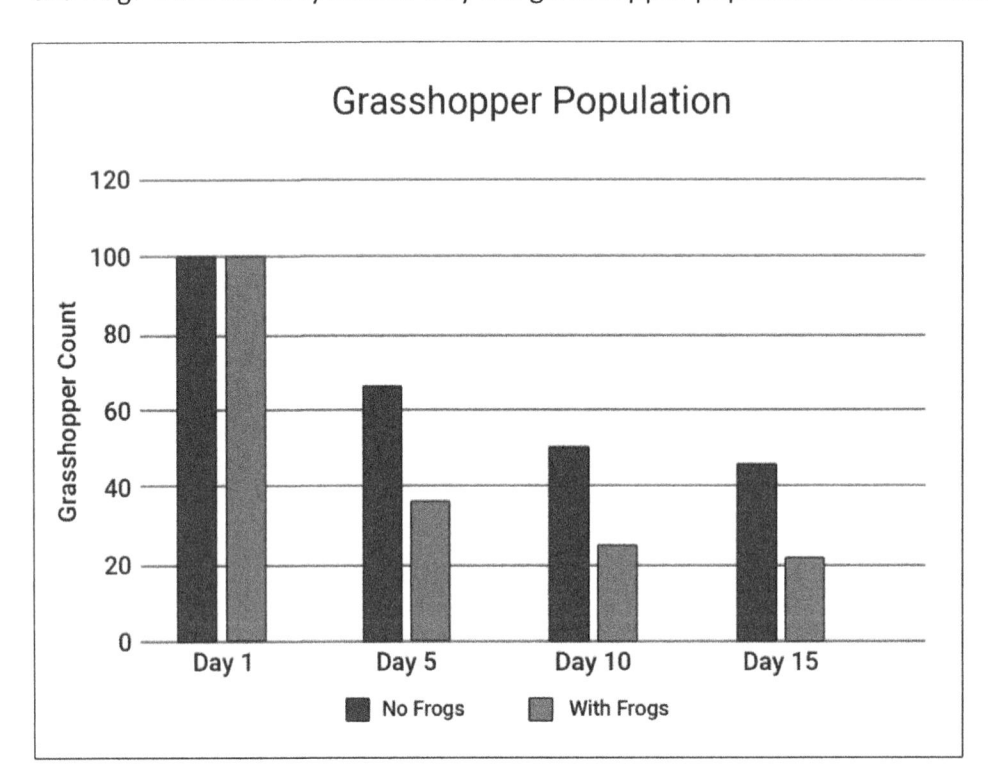

Which choice describes information from the graph that would weaken the student's conclusion?

- A. Both sections of the backyard started with 100 grasshoppers.
- B. The grasshopper population in the section of the backyard with frogs saw a sharp reduction between days 1 and 5.
- C. The grasshopper population in the section of the backyard without the frogs also saw a considerable decline over the 15 days.
- D. On day 15, the section of the backyard with no frogs had a higher grasshopper population than the section of the backyard with frogs.

As I tell my students, you want to think about, "what 'story' is the data telling?" So let's see if we can spot a trend or a pattern. As the days go by, the grasshopper population certainly decreases in the area with the frogs. However, it also decreases in the area with no frogs! This indicates that frogs were not the *only* reason why the grasshopper population would have declined. The answer is C.

Just looking at the other choices, choice A is true, but it has nothing to do with weakening the student's conclusion. Choices B and D would actually *help* the student's conclusion.

A Quick Recap

- Cover the answers to predict the word!
- Also try to predict the next idea.
- For some questions, read the question first.
- Summarize with a *verb* in mind.
- Let the answer choices "announce" the grammar rule.
- Look for trends or patterns in the data.

And Some Other Quick Tips for the Verbal Questions

- Remember, the verbal questions will appear in "clumps". For example, all of the transition questions will appear together, just like all of the punctuation questions will appear together, etc. This allows you to focus on one task at a time.
- The verbal questions follow a "sawtooth" pattern of difficulty. As you work through each set, the questions will get harder. Then, when you start the new type of question, it resets and goes back to easy. So for example, as you work through the sentence completion questions, you'll notice that they'll get harder. But after you finish the sentence completion questions, the first reading question that follows should be a little easier. And from there, they'll start to get harder again until the new type of question begins, etc.
- Make sure to read the full passage, even if the passage only asks about a specific detail. Often, you need to see how a certain detail affects other information in the passage.
- If you're pressed for time, make sure to knock out any "quick points". For example, you can probably work through the punctuation questions more quickly than the rhetorical synthesis questions. Somewhere around the 5-minute mark, bounce around to any "quick points" to answer as many questions as you can in the time that remains.
- And don't sweat any killer passage or killer question! It might be the experimental question that doesn't count.

We made it through every type of verbal question, good job!

Grab a snack.

Now let's dive into some great strategies for the math questions.

Chapter 13: Your Math Section Toolbox

"Daniel possesses an expert level of understanding when it comes to the math sections of the SAT and ACT. His methods help students to efficiently navigate the particularly difficult problems, thus bringing out their strengths."

— Jack C. (Class of 2020)

In this chapter, we'll cover some of the best tips for the math sections of the SAT and ACT. These are great approaches for when you get stuck on the algebraic "high school" approach.

Quick Domain Recap

In Chapter 3, we mentioned how the math questions are arranged throughout each module. Reread that section as needed.

Just like the verbal questions, the math questions are also categorized into four domains.

Domain 1:   Algebra
Domain 2:   Advanced Math
Domain 3:   Problem-Solving and Data Analysis
Domain 4:   Geometry and Trigonometry

We've talked about how the verbal questions are "clumped" together. For example, all of the sentence completion questions are grouped together, just like all of the rhetorical synthesis questions are grouped together, etc. This is not the case in the math section. The math questions are not grouped by domain.

Also, the math questions get harder as you move through the section. This might not be on an exact question-by-question basis. Still, the difficulty will escalate as you move from the start to the end of each module.

Here are some great strategies to help you navigate the math sections.

"Cheating" When the Answers Have Numbers

Ok, no, it's not really "cheating". I'll just call it a "fun" math approach. Or a "trick" if you prefer. Here's a question that often stumps my students.

Q. Joe went to the store, where cakes cost $10 and pies cost $5. If Joe spent $250 total, and bought 5 more pies than cakes, how many cakes did he buy?

- A. 11
- B. 12
- C. 13
- D. 14
- E. 15

This question could be done with a let statement or a system of equations. If you know how to solve it that way, great! However, many of my students struggle to set that up. So let's take another approach.

Look at the answers. They're all numbers. *One of these answers has to be right*. So, if we were to do a little guess-and-check with these numbers, sooner or later, one of them would have to give us $250. **When you have all numbers in the answer choices, you can use those numbers and work backwards!**

Now, this is where my students like to ask me, "But Daniel, doesn't that take too long?"

No.

Look at how the numbers are listed. On a standardized test, the answers will always be in numeric order. In this case, from least to greatest. So the question becomes, what's the best choice to start at?

Some students like to tell me the smallest answer. Others say the largest. Others say the one in the middle.

But you want to start with choice B. Huh? Stay with me.

If choice B gives you $250, then it's right! No need to continue.

However, if choice B gives you something more than $250, it means that we are already too high. *Therefore, the answer must be choice A.*

But now let's think about it the other way. If choice B gives you something *less than* $250, it means that choice B is too small. This means that choices A and B are out. You need a higher number. So which choice should you then test?

Choice D! Why? If choice D gives you $250, ding ding ding. The answer would be D. But if choice D is now too big, the answer must be C. And if choice D is too small, the answer must be E.

So, by testing choice B, you only need to test two of the five choices! (And if the answer is either A or B, you only need to test one.)

Pretty cool!

Now, in case any of that was confusing, let's do it for real. We're going to pretend that the answer is B.

If choice B is right, it means that Joe has 12 cakes and… how many pies? The question tells us that he has 5 more pies than cakes. So 12 cakes would mean 17 pies. And from there, they tell us that he's spending $10 per cake and $5 per pie. So let's see if we get $250 from all of that.

$$
\begin{aligned}
\text{cakes + pies} &= 250? \\
12\,(\$10) + 17\,(\$5) &= 250? \\
120 + 85 &= 250? \\
205 &= 250?
\end{aligned}
$$

We are looking for 250. Using choice B, we get 205. So we definitely know that B is not the right answer. But what else do we know? *We know that B is too small!* We need a higher answer choice to produce a higher final number. So not only can we eliminate choice B; we can also eliminate choice A.

Now we test choice D. Choice D means that he had 14 cakes. From there, remember, he has 5 more pies that cakes. So 14 cakes would mean 19 pies. And from there, you can incorporate the money. Let's see if we get $250.

$$
\begin{aligned}
\text{cakes + pies} &= 250? \\
14\,(\$10) + 19\,(\$5) &= 250? \\
140 + 95 &= 250? \\
235 &= 250?
\end{aligned}
$$

We wanted 250, but we got 235. We're still too low! We still need a higher number. That means the answer is E.

And you don't even need to test it! Pretty cool.

This is everything your high school teacher math doesn't want you to do. However, it's a perfectly good way to approach a standardized test question!

Again, this question could have been done algebraically. And if you know how to approach it that way, great. *However, if you can't, it doesn't mean that you can't answer the question!* There are often other ways into a standardized test question.

And just a quick side note, math questions on the ACT will contain five choices. Math questions on the SAT only list four choices. Still, you can use the same strategy for both of starting with choice B. So let's try one on now with only four choices.

Q. A jar contains 33 marbles, which are red, yellow, or green. If there is one more yellow marble than half of the number of red marbles, and twice as many green marbles as yellow marbles, how many red marbles are there?

   A. 12
   B. 14
   C. 16
   D. 18

I'll be here, moving my laundry from the washer to the dryer.

(Keep reading when you're done... or when you need help... whichever comes first.)

We're going to start with B. Choice B means that there are 14 red marbles. From there, they tell us that there is one more yellow marble than half of the number of red marbles. So if we have 14 red marbles, that will give us 8 yellow marbles.

Then they tell us that there are twice as many green marbles as yellow marbles. So 8 yellow marbles would give us 16 green marbles.

Are we right? They tell us that there are 33 total marbles. So let's see what these numbers add up to. 14 red + 8 yellow + 16 green = 38 total marbles.

So we didn't get 33. We know the answer is not choice B. But what else do we know? *Choice B gave us an answer that was too big!* We're already too high. This means that we need a smaller number; the answer must be A!

And no need to test it. Beautiful.

This is a great approach when you have all numbers in the answers. Test choice B. From there, if you need to, test choice D.

Now let's look at another strategy when you have all variables in the answer choices.

"Cheating" When the Answers Have Variables

Again, no, it's not "cheating". Just another fun math "trick". Here's an example.

Q. The expression $x^3 + x^6$ is equivalent to which of the following?

   A. x^9
   B. $2x^9$
   C. x^{18}
   D. $x^3(1 + x^2)$
   E. $x^3(1 + x^3)$

This question could also be done algebraically, but let's say that you're stumped with that approach. **When you see all variables in the answer choices, you can plug in your own numbers! From there, see which answer choice produces the same value.**

To illustrate, let's pick a number. You can pick anything you want, as long as you do your math correctly. Just to keep things simple, let's have $x = 2$. By plugging in 2:

$$x^3 + x^6 = 2^3 + 2^6 = 8 + 64 = 72$$

So if $x = 2$, the expression in the question gives us 72. That means that if we plug in 2 for every x in the choices, one of them will also have to give us 72!

I'll save you the trouble of doing for every choice; the answer is E. But just to prove it:

E. $\quad x^3(1 + x^3) = 2^3(1 + 2^3) = 8(1 + 8) = 8(9) = 72$

Choice E gives us 72. Winner winner chicken dinner!

So, when you see all variables in the answer choices, plug a number into the question. From there, see which answer produces the same value.

Let's do it again. I won't help on this one.

Q. The expression $\frac{6x+2}{2x-1}$ is equivalent to which of the following?

A) $\quad 3x - 2$

B) $\quad 3x - 1$

C) $\quad 3 + \frac{2x+1}{2x-1}$

D) $\quad 3 + \frac{5}{2x-1}$

And for purposes of keeping things simple, let $x = 2$ again. I'll be over here folding my laundry.

(Another sock gone rogue.)

Did you get choice C? I'm not saying yes, I'm not saying no. Let's check your math….

If you plug 2 into the given expression:

$$\frac{6x+2}{2x-1} = \frac{6(2)+2}{2(2)-1} = \frac{12+2}{4-1} = \frac{14}{3}$$

And if you plug 2 into choice C, you will indeed get 14/3 as well.

But here's the fun part…if you plug 2 into choice D, you will also get 14/3! (I won't even make you do the math; just trust me.)

Two answers? How can that be???

This is where this strategy gets a little dicey. You have to test all of the choices! Why? Because sometimes, more than one answer might come back as working. *If that happens, pick new numbers. Then, only test the remaining answers.*

And I won't even have you do the math. If you were to pick another number and just test choices C and D, only choice D would work. The answer is D.

But the bigger point: *just because choice C gave you 14/3 doesn't necessarily mean that it's the answer!* It's rare, but sometimes, more than one answer choice might produce the value you're looking for.

So, when you see all variables, picking numbers is a great strategy. *However, you must test every choice.* From there, if more than one choice works, pick new numbers.

Let's look at another type of question where picking numbers is a great approach.

Scalar Comparisons (Or "Bill's Copper Cylinder")

Q-a.   What happens to the perimeter of a square when you double its side?

Q-b.   What happens to the area of a square when you double its side?

Some of my students like to tell me the answer is, "They get bigger". Well, yes, but let's do better than that.

Other students tell me, "They will both double". Well... maybe.

Again, we can pick numbers! We gave 2 a lot of love on the last two questions, so let's throw 3 into the mix.

Draw a square with sides of 3. What is the perimeter of that square? For perimeter of a square, you have to multiply the sides by 4. 3 x 4 = 12.

Now let's find the area of that square. For area of a square, you have to square the side length. $3^2 = 9$.

So a square with sides of 3 will have a perimeter of 12 and an area of 9. Let that hang out for a moment.

Now the questions tell us to double the sides. So draw a new square, but this time, double the sides from 3 to 6.

The new perimeter would be 6 x 4 = 24. The new area would be $6^2 = 36$.

Let's compare those numbers to what we got the first time: the perimeter went from 12 to 24, while the area went from 9 to 36.

So what happened to the perimeter of the square when we doubled the sides? *We did indeed double it!* But what happened to the area of a square when we doubled its side? *We multiplied it by 4!*

And this is a classic type of SAT question. They love to ask how changing one dimension will affect another dimension. *Sometimes,* they will change by the same factor. *But not all the time!* In order to work around that, pick numbers!

Let's do it again. I'll give you a minute for this one. (And they do give you the formula for volume of a cylinder on the reference table, so I'll tell you that it's $V = \pi r^2 h$.)

Q. Bill has a copper cylinder. What will happen to the volume of the cylinder if he doubles the radius?

A. It will stay the same
B. It will multiply by 2
C. It will multiply by 4
D. It will multiply by 8

I'll be here, trying to solve The Case of the Missing Sock.

(Nope, not in the dryer.)

You can pick whatever number you like for the radius. Just to keep the numbers simple, let's go back to our friend 2. If we use that for the radius in the volume formula:

$$V = \pi r^2 h$$
$$V = \pi (2)^2 h$$
$$V = \pi (4) h = 4\pi h$$

And now they tell us to double the radius. So if we go from a radius of 2 to a radius of 4:

$$V = \pi r^2 h$$
$$V = \pi (4)^2 h$$
$$V = \pi (16) h = 16\pi h$$

So doubling the radius actually *quadrupled* the volume! The answer is C.

Again, changing one dimension by a certain factor won't necessarily change another dimension by the same factor. Picking numbers is a great way to work around that. (And remember how I said that I come up with silly little "names" for each type of question? I call that one Bill's Copper Cylinder. My students know that title very well.)

For more practice with these first few strategies, check out my video here!

https://tinyurl.com/DanFisch25

And staying on the picking numbers train, here's another favorite of the test.

Combined Percents (or "The Laptop")

Q.   A store takes 10% off the original price of a laptop. No one buys it, so the store takes off another 10%. The laptop now costs what percent of its original price?

9 out of 10 students will tell me that the store took off 20%, so now there's 80% left. But that's not the answer! Why?

This is another great time to pick numbers. And for percents, pick 100 to start.

So let's say that the laptop starts at $100. (Don't worry that it's not realistic. The math will still work.) They tell us to take 10% off the price. To find 10% of 100: 100 x .1 = 10. Taking $10 off of $100 would get us down to $90.

Now we're taking off another 10%. But here's the important part: *we're not taking 10% off the original $100! We're taking 10% of the new amount of $90.*

So to find 10% of 90: 90 x .1 = 9. This means we're taking $9 off of $90, which would get us down to $81. We've gone from $100 to $81.

And this is why it was so great to start at 100! This automatically tells you what percent of the original you are left with. The answer is 81%.

This is a combined percent question. For these questions, *you cannot simply add (or subtract) the percents.*

In other words, if I told you that a given value went up 5%, and then up another 5%, *it does not mean that it increased 10%.* Why? Because when you take 5% the second time, *you're taking it from a new number.*

Picking numbers is a great tool here as well! And specifically for percents, pick 100.

(My students know to call this one "The Laptop". Very popular!)

One more...

Thinking Algebraically (or "Widgets")

Before we do the next one, I'll give you the formula for exponential growth:

$$y = a(1+r)^t$$

In that formula, *y* represents the final amount, *a* represents the initial amount, *r* represents the rate, and *t* represents the time. And just as a heads up, you always have to convert the rate to a decimal.

Let's see how this might be tested on a question,

Q-a. Samantha starts with 1,986 grams of a substance. She adds a chemical that makes it grow 12% every week. Write an expression that represents the amount that remains after *w* weeks.

All we have to do is plug this data into the formula above. 1,986 is the starting amount, *w* is the time, and 12% is the rate. (And remember, we have to convert that to a decimal!)

So, plugging all of that in: $y = a(1+r)^t = 1986(1+.12)^w = 1986(1.12)^w$

Not too tough. But now let's kick it up a notch.

Q-b. Kristen starts with 28 grams of a substance. She adds a chemical that makes it grow 13% every 3 days. Write an expression that represents the amount that remains after *d* days.

This is basically the same question. 28 will be the initial amount and 13% will be the rate. But what do we do for the power of time if it grows 13% every 3 days... over *d* total days?

To help you with that, let's take a little detour to talk about something I call *widgets*.

Our brains have trouble processing variables. However, our brains are very good at processing numbers!

The golden rule: do unto variables as you would do unto numbers.

Huh? I'll explain.

If I told you that over the course of 12 days, something happened every 4 days, how many times did it happen?

You're probably rolling your eyes. 3 times, duh. But how did you get that? 12/4. *You took the total amount of time and divided it by how often it happened.*

Simple enough with numbers. But now let's try it algebraically. If I told you that over the course of *t* days, something happened every *b* days, how many times did it happen?

This is a bit harder. So if it helps you, go back to the 12 and the 4! If over the course of 12 days, something happened every 4 days, you were able to divide 12/4 to give you 3. And we can do the same thing with t and b! If over the course of t days, something happened every b days, it means that it happened t/b times.

So, let's apply that to Kristen in the example above. Over the course of d days, something happens every 3 days. How many times did it happen? d/3! That's the unit of time in the exponent. So the final answer would say:

$$y = 28(1.13)^{\frac{d}{3}}$$

So, whenever they tell a story with variables, pretend that they are numbers!

Let's practice that one more time.

Q-a.   If you buy w widgets that cost d dollars each, how much money did you spend?

If you're stuck, think of numbers! I'll make up some simple ones. Let's say that you have 5 items that cost $4 each. What did you spend? 5 x $4 = $20.

So do the same thing here. If you have w widgets that cost d dollars each, you would multiply those values. That means you spent wd.

But let's make that a bit harder.

Q-b.   If w widgets cost a total of d dollars, what is the price of each widget?

Once again, pick numbers! So let's say that you bought 6 items and spent a total of $18. What's the cost of each item? $3. But why? *Because you had to divide the total dollar amount by the number of items.*

So do the same thing with the variables! If w widgets cost a total of d dollars, it means that each widget cost d/w.

And this is the nature of algebraic thinking. When you get stumped with variables, pretend they are numbers. Substituting numbers in for variables can make an abstract concept much more approachable.

(And yes, my students know to call this "widgets". It's all about spotting your cousin questions!)

For more examples of modeling a situation, check out this video here.

https://tinyurl.com/DanFisch26

And for more practice with "widgets" and thinking algebraically, check out this guy!

https://tinyurl.com/DanFisch27

Now, are there algebraic approaches to the questions above? Yes. Are they always necessary? NO!!! These are great strategies to help you sidestep complicated algebra.

My students find these strategies incredibly helpful. Give them a shot on your next practice test!

Part IV: Other Things to Consider

"Daniel tutored all three of my girls, with nine years between the oldest and youngest. As the years progressed and the world changed, the SAT changed as well. Still, we could always count on Daniel to be a reliable source for up-to-the-minute information. This was especially helpful, given the ever-shifting nature of the testing landscape. Daniel was always there to help guide our girls through this process. Now that it's all in a book, it's a blessing to all students who can benefit from it! Best of luck to all studying."

— Laura M. (Mother of Students in the Classes of 2012, 2015 and 2020)

In the final part of this book, let's move away from academic lessons and talk about other aspects of test prep. I'll start with a few fun myths I often hear from my students. Then we'll move on to some other things to consider.

Chapter 14: Ten Myths About the SAT and ACT

"Everything you read on the internet is true."

— Abraham Lincoln

Over the years, I've heard some – how shall I say this – interesting rumors from my students about the SAT and ACT. They have heard one suggestion from a guidance counselor, something else from online research, and another opinion from Aunt Susan.

I'm sure all of these advice-givers meant well. Having said that, I often hear conflicting information about the tests. Some is misguided; some is just wrong.

So in this chapter, let's clear up some popular misconceptions about the SAT and ACT.

Myth 1: You "Have To" Submit All of Your Scores

Myth: Students often tell me that they "have to" submit all of their test scores to colleges.

Reality: Nope. See Chapter 10 for more details. But briefly: when the time comes to submit your scores to colleges, it is up to you to decide which test dates you want to send. However, that does come with certain caveats. Reread Chapter 10 as needed.

Myth 2: The "More Than Three Times" Rumor

Myth: As an extension of that first myth, some students have also told me, "If I take the test more than three times, *then* I have to submit the scores to colleges."

Reality: Still no. I have had students take the test more than three times, and then submit only one set of scores. The decision to send the scores is always up to you. It doesn't matter how many times you take the test.

Myth 3: Superscore Confusion

Myth: Some students think the superscore option lets them submit *just* their verbal numbers from one month, along with *just* their math numbers from another month.

Reality: When you submit the scores from any given month, you are submitting *all* of the scores from that month. Revisit Chapter 10 for the full details.

Myth 4: Standardized Test Prep is All About "Tricks"

Myth: Students and parents love to ask me things like, "It's all about test-taking tricks, right?"

Reality: Test prep is about learning material that you haven't seen in school. (Or material that you have seen, but oh heck, it's been a while.)

Granted, we have talked about some "tricks" in this book. In Chapter 11, for example, we covered some essential test taking strategies (how to navigate the sections, what to do when you're short on time, etc.) In Chapter 12, we talked about different strategies for the verbal questions (predicting your own answer first, summarizing with a verb, etc.) In Chapter 13, we saw some great alternate math strategies (plugging in numbers for variables, using the answer choices to work backwards, etc.)

These strategies are extremely helpful. That said, the majority of the time I spend with students is teaching them the actual material that is on the test. It's not about gamesmanship or tricks.

We've touched on some of this material already. And my channel covers even more of this content! Check it out. Here's a link to a particularly challenging math concept that comes up on the test. This one stumps many of my students, so give it a watch.

https://tinyurl.com/DanFisch28

Myth 5: The Test is "Easier" in a Certain Month

Myth: I also hear the tests are "easier" in certain months and "harder" in other months.

Reality: No.

Myth 6: It's Easier to Improve My Score on (Insert Name of Test Here)

Myth: Some students tell me how they should take the SAT, or how "everyone does better on the ACT".

Reality: There is no definitive answer that one test is better for everyone. Check out Chapter 5, where I cover the full details of how to decide between the SAT and ACT. The short answer – it depends. Also, check out Chapter 9, where I cover what you can expect in terms of reasonable score jumps on each.

Myth 7: Bad Reading Tips

I am sometimes playing relief pitcher for a student, so to speak, after they've already worked with another tutor or a class. These students sometimes tell me about dicey reading strategies they were taught.

Here are strategies that I've seen in print as part of a formal test prep curriculum.

Myth: You don't have to read the full passage. All you have to do is check the lines that a question refers to.

Reality: No! Ok fine, this might work once in a while. But it's certainly not the primary strategy you should follow. Let's say an ACT question asks, "What is the purpose of line 37?" If the purpose of line 37 was to contradict the preceding paragraph, or to establish an idea that will be supported in the next paragraph, you would not know that from just reading line 37.

Myth: You don't need to read entire paragraphs. All you have to do is read the first and last sentence of each paragraph.

Reality: This would be fantastic if every paragraph started with a nice topic sentence that announced the main idea. Likewise, it would be great if the last sentence of every paragraph summarized what you just read.

However, the passages are more sophisticated than that. The main idea of each paragraph is often hidden somewhere in the middle. And even more often, the main purpose is not explicitly stated. It is up to you as the reader to infer what an author is really trying to say. It won't always be spelled out for you in the first or last sentence.

Myth: You don't need to read the full passage. All you have to do is read the first and last paragraph of any passage.

Reality: Same speech as above – nope.

Sometimes, a passage might start with a brief anecdote. Other times, it might start with a concession statement that actually gives you the *opposing side* of the author's argument.

Whatever the case, this strategy does not work. There are no magical tricks for being able to decipher a passage by only reading a portion of it. So I'm sorry to disappoint, but you do need to read the entire passage.

And just a few more fun nuggets I've seen in different test prep books:

When in doubt – pick the answer with the most complicated word.

When stuck between two answers, pick the vague word.

When you don't know the answer, pick the word that you don't recognize.

You can't trust that the unfamiliar word in the answer choices will always be correct.

As we covered in Chapter 12, this is why it's so important to predict your own answer before you look at the choices! From there, see which choice best matches your prediction. And if you don't know what some of the choices mean, that's ok! Eliminate those that don't match your prediction.

From there, if the only remaining choice is the one with the strange word, then yes, pick it. But definitely don't pick a choice just because it contains a strange word.

Myth 8: When in Doubt – Pick Choice C

Myth: If you don't know what answer to put, choice C is the best answer.

Reality: Any answer will have the same statistical probability. 1 out of 4. (Or on the ACT math questions, 1 out of 5.) So if makes you feel better to pick choice C, sure. It's no better or worse than any other choice.

Guidance Counselors are Not Test Prep Experts!

This next anecdote isn't a widespread rumor. In fact, I only heard it from one client. However, it was so egregious, I had to include it.

Back in Chapter 5, I mentioned how certain test dates give you the option to analyze your questions from the exam. For the SAT, it was called the QAS report, which stood for Question and Answer Services. (I'm using the past tense because it seems to be going away for the digital test?) For the ACT, it's called the TIR report, which stands for Test Information Release (and I'm using the present tense there because the TIR report is thankfully sticking around!) Check out Chapter 5 for the schedule of when these reports are offered, and how to incorporate them into your test prep.

Unfortunately, the TIR report is only offered during certain months. For the other months, you'll get to see your scores, but not the questions.

So it seems like a no-brainer. Who wouldn't want this option? Well...

One year, the parents of one of my students told me that their guidance counselor told them... wait for it... *specifically not to order their questions from the test.*

After I came back from my coronary, I asked them why? Evidently, the guidance counselor told them that these reports, and I'm just quoting here, "...do not help. All the student does is memorize those answers for the next round."

(Insert Michael Scott screaming "no" repeatedly. Go look it up on YouTube. I'll wait.)

These reports give you vast amounts of valuable information. You can see where you made a careless error, where you're running out of time, and above all, what material you still need to learn! Maybe you've never learned this grammar rule over here, or maybe you forgot that math formula over there. These reports are a critical part of your test prep plan.

It's not about memorizing your answers from just one specific question; it's about recognizing what *brand* of question you're missing so you can spot it again on an upcoming test. (See Chapter 7 for my speech on "brand recognition".)

So if anyone ever tells you not to utilize the TIR report for the ACT (or if it comes back, the QAS report for the SAT), smile politely and ignore that advice.

And once again, let's all pray for the return of the QAS reports.

Myth 9: These Exams Cover What You're Learning in School

Myth: The SAT and ACT tests claim to cover the same material that you see in high school.

Reality: Nope. Reread Chapters 1 and 4.

Myth 10: These Exams Cover the What is Relevant in Life

Myth: Both test companies profess that these exams cover the material that will help students beyond the classroom.

Reality: Nope. Reread Chapters 1 and 4.

I'll repeat my favorite meme from those chapters.

> *"I'm glad I learned about parallelograms instead of how to do my taxes. It really comes in handy during parallelogram season."*

Oh fine, I'll make a concession here for those who think I'm just being a Negative Nancy. Will *some* of the material on the SAT and ACT be relevant beyond the classroom? Yes.

Here's a text that one of my students sent her mother when she got to college.

> "I am taking a class called Writing for Mass Communications. We've been talking about grammar, and it all seems pretty easy because I already learned it with Daniel! But there are people in this class who have no idea how to write a proper sentence. Thank you for getting me the SAT tutor; it helped me with a lot more than just testing."

Thanks, Sarah!

Here's another testimonial from a recent student.

> "Daniel is the sole reason for my success on the grammar portions of the SAT exam. However, his teachings did not stop once my exam book closed. I am now in law school and use his teachings every day!"

Thanks John!

So yes, some of these topics (especially the grammar rules) will come up later in life, depending on your choice of vocation.

But, as I joked in an earlier chapter, will it ever help you in life to know how the discriminant of a parabola affects the nature of the roots? Never.

Is it something the test wants you to know? Yes.

And can I help you with it? You bet!

(And for those who need help with that topic, I cover it in this video. Check it out!)

https://tinyurl.com/DanFisch29

Chapter 15: Testing with Accommodations

"Daniel's methods will provide you with the most precious asset on test day: time."

— Jill G. (Mother of Students in the Classes of 2012 and 2015)

Many of my students require testing accommodations. These accommodations might include getting extra time, sitting in a room without other students, or having a scribe. Other students often ask me how they can get accommodations for the test. This is a particularly popular question for students taking the ACT, where the timing factor is much more challenging.

So in this chapter, let's unpack these details.

Two Disclaimers

Two quick caveats before we start.

First – I am not a special education teacher or a school psychologist. My expertise deals with tutoring and test prep. That said, I've worked with hundreds of students over the years, many of whom were approved for testing accommodations based on their IEP or 504 plans. So my goal for this chapter is to offer some insight into this topic, based on what I've seen with those students.

Second – things are shifting as the digital test replaces the paper test! So suffice it to say, College Board might change this protocol as the digital test rolls out. These are the most current procedures at the time of this writing.

Types of Accommodations

There are many disabilities that might warrant certain types of testing accommodations. They are not limited to the following, but they might include ADHD, processing issues, dyslexia, visual impairment, anxiety, or a sudden injury.

For example, last year, I had a student who had a cast on his leg from a recent accident. He had orders from the doctor that he needed to stand up every so often. As such, he was allowed to take the test in a separate room so he wouldn't distract other students when he needed to get up to walk around.

And there are other types of accommodations as well, such as time and a half, double time, small group testing, a test-read option for students with visual impairments, and many others.

As you can see, the test makers do their best to accommodate the needs of a student. For that reason, they require professional documentation for approval. Let's talk about what that process entails for each test.

So Can You Just "Have Your Doctor Write a Note"?

If my students struggle with the timing factor (especially on the ACT), their parents sometimes ask me what they can do to get extra time.

This is a fair question. These parents aren't trying to game the system or gain an unfair advantage. They're just seeing what's possible. Still, it's not a feature you can just add to your registration. Those accommodations are meant for students who have documented needs. Or put more bluntly – you can't just ask your doctor to write a note you can then submit for time accommodations. The test companies require you to provide documentation of the need for accommodations in school.

Here's how it works to apply.

Putting Together Your Paperwork

The first step is to see if you are eligible for accommodations. In order to qualify, you need an assessment by a qualified professional indicating the need for an accommodation. Some accommodations might be documented by your school district. Others might require a credentialed specialist, such as a neuropsychologist, psychometrist, etc.

Whatever the case, a student needs to show documentation that the disability directly affects his or her performance on a standardized test. Likewise, the student needs to show a history of relevant accommodations in school.

Also, each test follows a different timeline for how current that documentation needs to be. For example, for students with ADHD, College Board requires valid testing be completed within five years of the test, while the ACT requires that it be within three years. For students with visual disabilities, College Board shortens that window to two years, while the ACT shortens that window to one year.

And there are other variations as well. Work with your guidance counselor to contact each testing company directly. They can help walk you through the process.

Submitting Your Request

Once you've gathered all of your necessary documentation, you can submit your request for accommodations.

As I mentioned, you might have obtained your diagnosis directly from your school district, or independently through a specialist. Each one follows its own timeline. If your documentation is sent through your school district, the process is typically expedited. If your documentation is sent through an independent learning specialist, it might take a few weeks longer.

Moving Forward with SAT Accommodations

At this point, each test follows a different procedure.

For the SAT, College Board will contact you directly. You will receive an Eligibility Letter, which tells you what type of accommodations you are approved for. You will also receive an SSD code (Services for Students with Disabilities), which you'll need whenever you sign up for the test. From there, you're able to register for the test.

Once College Board approves your accommodations, those accommodations are valid for all College Board assessments (the PSAT, the SAT, and the AP tests). In other words, once your accommodations are approved for one of these tests, you are automatically approved for the others. You don't need to submit separate requests.

With your accommodations in place, you can sign up for the test. Just make sure to have your SSD code when you do. You'll also need to bring your SSD Eligibility Letter to your testing center, along with your other registration materials.

And just a brief sidenote: some students have accommodations that allow them to take the test on paper rather than digitally.

The timing of the paper test is a bit longer than that of its digital counterpart. Why? Remember – the digital test is adaptive. A student's performance in an earlier module will dictate what he or she sees in a later module. This helps to pinpoint the score more quickly.

But a paper test, of course, can't adapt as the student takes it. For that reason, the paper test sections are a bit longer. This gives College Board more information to calibrate the scores more accurately.

If you have paper testing accommodations, you can find practice paper tests online, as well as in the College Board book. See Chapter 5 for the full details of which tests appear there, as well as a link for where you can purchase it.

Moving Forward with ACT Accommodations

For the ACT, it's a little different. You actually don't hear back about your accommodations until you register for a test.

In other words, you first have to sign up for a test date. When you do, you either have to pick an option called National Extended Time, or another called Special Testing. National Extended Time includes 50% extra time, also called time and a half. Special Testing includes everything else (double time, special testing locations, etc.).

Once you sign up for a date, you'll receive an email to send to the Testing Coordinator (TC) at your school.

If you are approved, your TC will be notified. If you are taking National Extended Time, you'll have the option to use the same accommodations moving forward. Bring your registration ticket with your National Extended Time designation. If you're taking the Special Testing, the Testing Coordinator will help you sign up for the next testing window.

If Your Accommodations Are Denied

If your requests for accommodations are denied, you can submit an appeal. Your appeal should specify the documentation that was missing. Work with your guidance counselor or your TC. The appeal will take a few more weeks to process.

Some Pros... and a Few Cons

The big pro of getting approved is, of course, getting the accommodations you need! Whether that's extra time or testing in a room by yourself, your accommodations will help you perform to the best of your potential. So that's obviously a big plus.

Also, my students sometimes ask me if their accommodations will be held against them in some way. For example, I recently had a student ask me if a college would look down on him for taking the test with extended time. Don't worry about that! When you submit your scores to colleges, you are only sending the scores themselves. Colleges won't know what sort of accommodations you had while taking the test.

Granted, you can choose to disclose a certain disability in other parts of your application. This can help you get approved for similar accommodations in college. But your test scores themselves won't reflect any information about what sort of accommodations you had while taking the test.

Still, let's talk about some potential drawbacks. First is the endurance factor. If you have extended time, it turns the test into a longer mental marathon. Students who are approved for time and a half could be there for more than five hours.

However, if you're taking the test with double time, you won't take the full test in one sitting. Instead, they extend the test over two days. You'll take a few sections on one day, and a few sections on another day. This potentially means missing a day of school in order to take the test. (Granted, some of you might put that in the pro column! Fair enough.) But do keep in mind, double time means sitting for the test over the course of several days.

Also, once your accommodations are approved, make sure to follow those parameters for any practice tests! That way, you can work on your endurance and focus. This is especially important if you have double time; you'll need to carve out two days to sit for a practice test, not just one day.

And there is one more potential drawback to consider.

In Chapter 5, I talked about the best times of the year to take the test. Specifically, I talked about the TIR reports for the ACT. This feature allows you to analyze your questions from your test, but they are only offered for certain test dates. See chapter 5 for the full details. The TIR reports are an integral part of your testing timeline.

However, students with certain accommodations don't necessarily have the option to order their TIR reports for the ACT.

If you take the test with time and a half on the same Saturday as everyone else, you typically will get your TIR report. However, if you're taking the Sunday test (for religious reasons or otherwise), you'll only have access to your TIR report for the April exam. And if you participate in Special Testing (double time or taking the test later that week), then you won't have access to your TIR report at all.

Why? Because you're not taking the same test as everyone else. The test companies do this to prevent cheating. They assume that students will talk about the questions right after the test. (Which mine always do!) So students who take the test a few days later will not see the same test that was just given on Saturday. The ACT folks don't release the TIR reports for those alternate test dates.

Now, don't get me wrong; *this is not a reason to forgo your accommodations!* Don't give up your accommodations just so you can analyze your TIR reports. *If you need your accommodations, please, use them.* But do keep in mind depending on what type of accommodations you have, you might not get to analyze your test questions using the TIR report.

It's a minor concession that shouldn't outweigh the benefits of taking the test with accommodations. Still, it's something worth mentioning.

(And just to echo what I said in Chapter 5 – please join me in prayer that the QAS reports will return for the SAT.)

Chapter 16: Things We Still Don't Know (For Now)

"I know that I know nothing."

— Socrates

As I've said throughout this book, this is a fluid situation; we are learning more about the digital SAT every day! And surely, more information will come to light in the coming years as the test goes through its growing pains. The information in this book is the most current data we have at the time of publication.

But many questions still exist. Here are some things we'll be keeping an eye on. And hopefully, many of them will be answered by the time you're reading this!

Stay tuned to my website www.fasttracktutoringllc.com, and I'll keep you posted as the newest information comes in on each of the following questions.

The QAS Reports

Are the QAS reports officially gone for good? If so, shame on College Board. See Chapter 5 for my full thoughts on this. We can all hope for their return….

The September TIR Report

Also from Chapter 5, the ACT always offered the TIR report in December, April, and June. For the 2023 – 2024 academic year, TIR report will now be available in *September*, April, and June. Why did they change it? I don't know. Will it stay that way for upcoming years? I don't know.

If it does, there will now be quite a gap between the September and April TIR reports. The test is offered between those months, but those test dates don't offer the TIR reports. So plan your timeline accordingly! Check out Chapter 5 for more details.

Test Timing

What exact dates will the digital SAT be offered? How many times a year? What about the School Day Testing option, where schools can administer the test during the week?

Hopefully, College Board will publish more of this information by the time you're reading this!

But staying on the topic of test timing – back in Chapter 4, I mentioned that the digital SAT will allow schools more flexibility as to when they can offer the exam. Because the test is now digital, schools won't have to give the exam on a specific date; they'll be able to choose a range of dates.

This already started with the 2023 digital PSAT. Some of my students, for example, took the digital PSAT on Wednesday, October 11th. Others took it on Saturday, October 14th. Others took it on Monday, October 16th.

One school even offered the PSAT over several different days. More specifically, the sophomores at this school sat for the PSAT on Wednesday, October 11th, while the juniors sat for it on Thursday, October 12th.

This begs an interesting question – is a similar thing going to happen with the digital SAT? And if so, will College Board offer *x* different tests on *x* different dates? And if not, what measures have they taken to prevent cheating from one test date to the next?

Does College Board have enough questions "in their bank" to give wholly original tests across several dates within the same month?

Or – might different tests on different days within a given month pull from *some* of the same questions?

Or – might the different tests on different days within a given month contain some identical sections (easy vs. hard modules notwithstanding)?

Let the record show, I don't have these answers. I'm just posing questions.

Now, in previous years, there were *four* different variations of the paper PSAT within the same month. Some students took the Wednesday PSAT. Others took the Saturday PSAT. Others took a different Wednesday date (particularly, those with religious conflicts). And students from other schools were occasionally selected to take an "alternate" PSAT exam. This test was given on the same Wednesday as that first one I mentioned, but these students saw a different test (even though it was given on the same date). So College Board did indeed offer four different versions of the paper PSAT within that month.

Will College Board do the same thing for the upcoming digital test? And if not – what does that mean about students "leaking" questions after they take one of the earlier dates in a given stretch? Surely, College Board must have considered this as a potential security threat to its test. We shall see when the digital tests start!

Score Results Timing

Students who took the paper SAT would typically see their scores 13 days after they took the exam. This was not a guarantee, but usually, the scores would be posted two Fridays after the exam.

College Board says that the digital test will shorten that timeline to "a matter of days".

That would be great!

That said, I had students outside of the United States take the digital SAT in the spring, summer, and fall of 2023. Those scores scores still took 13 days to appear online.

Granted, these were the very first digital tests to be given. So it's certainly possible College Board will improve its systems and shorten this timeline moving forward. We shall see!

Paper Test and Digital Test Superscoring

In Chapter 10, we discussed superscoring. Yet my spellcheck still hates it.

To quickly recap, superscoring is a policy that allows you to combine your best verbal numbers from one test with your best math numbers from another test. However, this comes with some stipulations; reread Chapter 10 as needed.

But here's an interesting wrinkle: how will superscoring work for students in the class of 2025 who take both the paper test as well as the digital test? Will colleges allow students to utilize the superscore option to combine their verbal numbers from one test format with the math numbers from the other?

I suspect the answer will be yes. The fancy phrase being bandied about the test prep industry is College Board "ensures parity between the two tests".

We will see if colleges allow superscoring between the two test formats.

Is a Digital ACT on the Way?

In Chapter 2, I mentioned how the ACT does offer a digital version of their test. However, the digital ACT test is identical to the current paper ACT test; it's just offered on a digital platform. At the time of this writing, there are no plans for the ACT to completely overhaul its format.

Stay tuned to my website for all of these questions! (And one final prayer for the QAS reports please.)

Chapter 17: Maintaining Perspective

"Working with Daniel was a game changer. I always felt that he was willing to go above and beyond to ensure that I felt confident on exam day – not an easy feat for a high school student juggling academics, sports, college applications, and a budding social life. He has an arsenal of materials, tips, and tricks that made studying for the exam much more palatable, even enjoyable. His in-depth approach challenged me, and my results were certainly better for it."

— Sydney L. (Class of 2014)

I know that preparing for your SAT and ACT tests can be extremely stressful. I often tell my students that I worked harder during my junior year of high school than I did during any year of college!

But I'm sure I don't need to tell you that. You're going through it now. As Sydney said in the quote above, you're balancing your test prep with your regular schoolwork, sports schedule, I.B. classes, A.P. classes, model congress, band practice, play rehearsal, part time jobs, social life, dance competitions, and heaven forbid… a little downtime.

So yeah, you have a lot going on!

At the end of the day, try to keep it all in perspective.

Channel Your Stress in a Positive Way

I won't give you generic advice like "don't be stressed!" First, that would be a bit naïve on my part. It's totally normal to be stressed with everything you have going on. Second, it's easy for me to tell you not to be stressed; I'm not the one going through the test prep process!

So I won't say it. What I *will* say is to try to channel that stress in a productive way. If you're feeling anxious about taking the test, that's actually good news! It means you're invested in your score. It also means that you're motivated to work on your test prep! Believe me, I can't say that about all of my students. (See Chapter 9 for some fun stories of my students who "checked out" early.)

All of that said, don't let that stress get the better of you….

Finding a Balance

You can probably tell by now, I'm a planner. After all, the name of my YouTube channel is *Plan Your Work – Work Your Plan*.

But I'll let the pendulum swing the other way for a moment. ***I don't ever want my students to feel their test prep is interfering with their emotional, physical, or mental health.***

Just to get serious for a moment, I've worked with students who were going through some serious stuff outside of our work together: the death of a close family member, parents going through a divorce, health issues, eating disorders, abuse, etc.

Not to mention, all of the factors I mentioned at the top of the chapter, a recent health crisis, and just the daily stress of being a teenager!

I have seen many students put an awful lot of pressure on themselves. Even if they saw significant score increases, they still felt like a failure if they didn't hit a certain number.

And this becomes a delicate balance. ***If you find that your test prep is wearing on you too much, stop. Your physical, mental, and emotional health are far more important than your test scores.***

Time On Your Side

Remember – you have time on your side! Obviously, the goal is to take the test as few times as necessary. But if you need to, you can take the test into the fall of your senior year. I've had students take the test as late as November or December of their senior year, depending on certain admissions deadlines.

If you can retire after your first shot, that's fantastic. But don't put any undue pressure on yourself. Especially if it's your first time in the room.

There is No Magic Number for Admission

Also, keep in mind what we said back in Chapter 6: good scores are relative. There are no guarantees.

It's never a situation where "scoring *x* and above means you're in" or "scoring *y* and below means you're out". Certain numbers just "put you in the conversation more". But there is no hard cutoff.

Your test scores are *a component* of your application, but they are not *the component* of your application. Admissions offices take a holistic approach, looking at test scores, GPA, the rigor of your course work, extracurricular activities, letters of recommendation, work experience, essays, etc.

On the pessimistic side, at a school like MIT, *everyone* might be applying with ACT math and science numbers in the 33 – 36 range. Other elite schools might reject applicants with perfect scores. A few years ago, I had a student with SAT numbers well into the 700 range for each section, along with an ACT score of 35. He was rejected from Berkley.

On the flip side of that, I could tell you many stories of my students getting accepted to colleges with test scores far below the median scores for that school.

So work hard to achieve your best possible test scores. Leave it all on the field so that you don't have any regrets. After that, it's beyond your control. Colleges will make their decisions based on many factors. Your test scores are only one piece of that puzzle.

And Celebrate the Score Jumps You See!

And make sure to celebrate your score jumps!

In Chapter 9, I covered what you might expect to see in terms of reasonable score jumps. Set realistic goals for yourself. Don't start the process with a mindset of "*x* or bust", or "I'm not done until I score *y*".

But no matter what the final numbers are, be proud of the score jumps that you do achieve!

Test Optional

And then there's the test optional movement I covered in Chapter 6. I want to be fully transparent on this point: these tests might not be necessary for every student! Check out that chapter for my full thoughts on this topic. Some schools no longer require test scores, but others do. And for other test optional schools, you'll still need test scores to earn certain scholarships, or for certain tracks within that school.

These Tests Do Not Define You

Above all, it's important to remember these tests do not define you. You are more than your SAT score, and you are more than your ACT score.

I've had students who struggle mightily with these tests. Still, I could tell they were great kids. *Your SAT and ACT scores don't reflect anything about your empathy, your work ethic, your kindness, or your character.*

These tests are a blip on your educational journey. Work hard to do your best, but don't let these tests dictate your sense of self-worth.

Plan Your Work – Work Your Plan

Let's go back to the story I told in the Introduction. I called that student Jackie. (I made up her name, but not the story.) The point of that story was not to emphasize her score jumps; it was to emphasize how she walked into the test with a new sense of confidence, knowing exactly what to expect.

And that's what test prep is about: going into the test knowing that you've done everything you can to prepare.

I'll end with this quote from a previous client.

> *"Daniel tutored all three of our sons. We appreciated his 'do the work and you can succeed' attitude. The sessions weren't always easy, but neither are the SATs. He gave our boys definitive steps to follow to achieve their personal academic best. That gave us the peace of mind that they were going into the test prepared and with a plan."*

And I've given you a great plan as well! To recap:

- Follow the steps from Part II.
- Utilize the strategies from Part III.
- Track your cousin questions to pinpoint the topics where you still need help. (See Chapter 7 for a full explanation of this process.)
- And use my videos to reinforce any shaky topics! I'll leave you with this one, which has some helpful tips on how to avoid careless errors on the test.

https://tinyurl.com/DanFisch30

More than anything, remember this: *all of these questions are the same*. You'll know you're making progress when you can look at a question and say, "Aha! That one is a 'cousin' of Australia's Bird", or "this is just another variation of Melissa's Balloon".

The best test-takers are by no means the "smartest". They are those who can identify the underlying principle of the question.

It's all about pattern recognition. "They're showing me A, so it's time to do B." This will help you recognize how all of these questions are the same.

Because they are!

It's been an honor and a privilege to bring this information to you. Especially to those who cannot afford expensive test prep. This book, and my YouTube channel, are intended to bridge the gap between what is not taught in school and what the tests want you to know. (Did I mention yet they don't teach this stuff in high school?)

I've given you great steps to plan your work – now it's time to work your plan.

Best of luck!

Acknowledgements

Neither my business nor this book would be here without the support of many people. They each deserve their own chapter. However, the SAT and ACT prefer concision.

First is my family. My deepest thanks to:

- My parents for supporting me with unbridled love and encouragement. Thanks to my dad for my left brain (and for giving me the nudge to call Kaplan for my first tutoring interview). Thanks to my mom for my right brain (and for talking me up among the townsfolk in the early days of client-scrounging). And thank you for not laughing when I first told you my crazy idea of incorporating my tutoring business. I love you both.
- My sister Amanda, who can not only play superhero mom, but can communicate in 80's movie quotes using only emojis. And thanks for taking me to T.G.I. Fridays with the cool high school kids when I was in 8th grade.
- My nephews Alex and Elliott for giving me a renewed sense of awe, joy, and vitality each and every day. I hope this book did not make you… "fall asleep". (Inside joke. It's ok if you're not laughing. They will be.)
- And Tony for your support, lasagna, tech guidance, and YouTube editing. And above all, for staying my brother through everything.

Next are my friends. Again, this section would be insufferable if I listed you all. You know who you are. But a special thanks to:

- Jordan and Lenae for the countless talks, hikes, theater visits (and occasional walk-outs), hot tub dips, business musings, Key West dive spots, Hell's Kitchen dinners, Mediterranean horizons, Kentucky bourbon trails, and Canadian Rocky therapy sessions.
- Jessica and Bret for always making me feel like family (and for the tough love brand of advice when I need it).
- And Rob and Melanie. Rob – thank you for always being the rational voice to my impulsive id. Melanie – thank you for being a wonderful friend, a shrewd business coach, and the smartest and most compassionate human I know.

And thank you to those who helped me write this book!

- Especially my Uncle Arty, who led me to Mick, who led me to Woody, who led me to Krystine. Thank you for all of your expertise in guiding me through this process.

- A big thank you to Erica Gordon-Mallin, who gave me the best Book Writing 101 crash course that a guy could ask for. I'm relenting on using two spaces between sentences, but I'm holding fast on my punctuation for farmers' market. The publishing world and Talula are both lucky to have you.
- My lawyer, John, for being the coolest guy in Southold. You're a gentleman and a poet of the highest order. I promise to give you props when *The Wall Street Journal* grants me an interview.
- Katie for all of the social media magic! And while we're at it, thanks to Nico and the Ground Central jammers for all of the music, inspiration, and caffeine.
- And Jillian for letting me talk through all possible permutations and combinations of this book. If anyone can appreciate the work it took me to get to this final draft, it's someone who will unabashedly open six bottles of wine until she finds the one that she wants.

And finally, a big thank you to:

- My clients. My business is nothing without you. I've never had to advertise because you all keep talking about me – a silly little detail that I never have taken for granted (nor ever will). Thank you for letting me into your homes and into your lives.
- You, the reader! I hope you found this information as helpful as my students do.
- Melanie Morgan. Your outstanding work was an integral part of helping me get my business off the ground. Tell Tiff that I'm practicing my knife skills for our next cooking night. (I'm getting better at using enough seasoning. You can always add, but you can't subtract.)
- And last, and perhaps most, Rich Silverstein. We solopreneurs are one-man-bands. Thank you for making me feel like I'm not alone in this crazy self-employed gig. Here's to your renewed health in the years ahead, my friend.

Client Testimonials

Disclaimer #1: All of the testimonials throughout this book refer to scores that were recorded from the current ACT test format, as well as those recorded from the *paper* SAT test format. Alas, this book was published *just before* the digital test came out in the U.S.

That said – see the beginning of Part III for the details of an international student I worked with who saw one of the first rounds of the digital test before it started in the U.S. She was able to improve her digital test scores from 1090 to 1250 on the Bluebook tests, and then 1260 on the June 2023 exam to 1400 on the October 2023 exam!

Disclaimer #2: Certain students and parents asked to remain anonymous for their testimonials, which is why I refer to some by their initials and others by their full names.

Disclaimer # 3: This section is 50% for you (to keep you motivated), and 50% for me (to make me feel better after a bad day)…

… maybe 40-60.

"Dan's methods are brilliant. He was able to break down the test and create effective strategies to tackle each section. As a result, he improved our scores significantly. We highly recommend this book! It is a gem."

— Bianca (mom) and Mikayla (Class of 2016)

"Both of my daughters worked with Dan preparing for the SAT and ACT. His methods are clear and very easy to follow. Both daughters had significant jumps in their scores and ended up in their dream schools with scholarships! Dan's book will be an invaluable tool for any child preparing for the college acceptance process."

— M.M. (Parent of Students in the Classes of 2016 and 2018)

"Daniel was so different from any other program or tutor that we'd worked with. After starting in the 900's on his PSAT, my son started working with Daniel. Once he started learning Daniel's amazing process, he improved his SAT score up to 1190, and then up to 1370! Plus, he was able to earn a Presidential Scholarship of $20,000 a year. I can't wait to suggest Daniel's book to anyone who wants to improve their scores."

— Meredith from New York (Parent of a Student in the Class of 2020)

"Daniel's insight into the SAT and ACT is second to none. After a handful of sessions, our daughter went from 1190 on her sophomore PSAT up to 1290 on her junior PSAT. Daniel's individualized approach helped her then go from 1330 on the October 2022 exam to 1490 on the March 2023 exam! To say that we are thrilled is an understatement. We recommend Daniel's book and are looking forward to working with him again to help prepare our sons."

— K.C. (Father of a Student in the Class of 2024)

"On my own, I was only able to take a step from the 1100's into the 1200's. Starting with Daniel, I took another step into the 1300's. Then, on the June 2022 exam, I scored a 1450!"

— Josue M. (Class of 2023)

"We were fortunate enough to have Daniel prepare both of our children for the stressful SATs. I would highly recommend Daniel's comprehensive book to any parents who are looking to improve their child's SAT scores. I wish we could have had unlimited access to Daniel's sessions. Now with this book, you can!"

— Rosanna and John H. (Parents of Students in the Classes of 2019 and 2017)

"Working with Daniel was amazing! He puts so much thought into teaching students what they do not learn in school. My daughter's scores helped her get into so many schools, along with scholarships. If he's putting his magic into a book, you should run out and buy it!"

— Jenna's Mom (Class of 2023)

"Daniel Fischer is amazing at what he does. He worked with both of my boys for their college entrance exams. I always thought he should write a book to share his 'tips and tricks' with a broader audience. Well... here it is!

Daniel is able to organize, simplify, and streamline the process of preparing for these exams. This makes the idea of prepping less daunting and ultimately helps the students to become more confident. I can't say enough good things about Daniel and his work."

— Tina C. (Mother of Students in the Classes of 2015 and 2018)

"Daniel worked with all three of our kids on their SAT and ACT exams. He's amazing! They all improved their scores dramatically after working with him. He knows all the 'tricks' and best ways to approach each section so your child can maximize his or her potential. I know his book will be a great tool in achieving your best scores."

— Bob and Donna R. (Parents of Students in the Classes of 2017, 2019, and 2021)

"Working with Daniel was the best decision we made for our children to prepare for the SAT. Follow his tips and your children are sure to increase their scores!"

— Ann T. (Mother of Students in the Classes of 2019 and 2022)

"Daniel Fischer is extremely knowledgeable about the SAT and the ACT. He has wonderful insights about tips, strategies, and time management. Most of all, he knows how to teach the material that kids don't see in school! My son saw significant score increases after working with Daniel. And now with this book, you can too! It's like your 'secret weapon' in test prep."

— A.Q. (Mother of a Student in the Class of 2021)

"Daniel tutored all four of our children over the span of eight years with great outcomes. His expertise was so impactful that we continued with our younger children, even after we had moved out of the state! Don't miss this opportunity to learn his methods."

— J. M. (Mother of Students from New York... then Ohio... then Connecticut...)

"Daniel worked with all three of my children over the course of six years. During that time, I recommended him to countless friends. I saw my children's confidence grow because they were thoroughly prepared; working with Daniel, they knew that they had developed the tools to be successful. Daniel's methods are extremely effective and his results are unparalleled."

— Anne McCabe (Mother of Students in the Classes of 2016, 2019 and 2023)

"We were fortunate to have Daniel mentor both our children for their SAT exams. We had heard family and neighbors rave about his process. Daniel went above and beyond our expectations; one of my children was three questions away from a perfect score and the other child dramatically increased his score following Daniel's instruction. The hardest part was getting Daniel; his calendar is very full. Super excited that everyone will now have access to his brilliance!"

— E.C. (Mother of Students in the Classes of 2017 and 2019)

About the Author

Daniel Fischer is the founder of F.A.S.T. Track Tutoring, LLC, a company focused on SAT and ACT test prep. Drawing on over 20 years of experience, he tailors his approach to each student's unique learning style. He is also the creator of the YouTube channel *Plan Your Work – Work Your Plan*, which helps students maximize their SAT and ACT scores. A graduate of Cornell University, Daniel wrote and hosted the on-demand cable program *Mastering the SAT*. Previously, he served as a tutor trainer and curriculum writer at Kaplan, Inc. He enjoys cooking, hiking, and crying over the New York Mets.

Made in the USA
Monee, IL
22 June 2024